THE ATHENADORAN LIBRARY

THE·DANAA
,
EPISTVLÆ·PHÆDRANÆ
,
TA·MEN·TAO
,
THE·RESCRIPTS

DANAAN PRESS

EY 5.3005 - 5.3039
Copyright © 1983, 1984, 1996, 2017 CE by Eduard J. Qualls.
Second Edition
All rights reserved. No part of the contents of this book may be reproduced or transmitted in any form or by any means without the express written permission of the copyright holder.

For the latest information on Danaan Press, its offerings, and on The Danaans and who we are and what we are doing, visit our website at
www.DanaanPress.com

Published by Danaan Press, Inc., in the United States of America.

ISBN: 978-1-890-000-07-3
DANAAN PRESS ID: 001-0810-02101-4

INTRODUCTION

The Athenadoran Library is the first full statement of the principles of the Danaan Religion and its championship of Goddess Devotion. It goes beyond the current corpus of Goddess-related writings, a corpus dominated by historical expositions, to put forth a synthesis of that history with Science, reason and sensibility, to produce a guide for modern life, a guide based on healthful attitudes, good psychology, and the unfettering of the human drives for peace, love and excellence.

This volume contains three, originally separate, works. Each of those was written and edited into its present form during the fifteen year period which started in EY 5.3000 (1978 CE). Each volume is in a different form, reflecting different ways of reaching out toward a shared goal, the shared goal of greater personal freedom.

The Danaa (pronounced like *Danaan* /da-ˈneː-ən/, but dropping the final '*n*': /da-ˈneː-ɐ/) represents the cumulative impact of Athenadorus's studies of the works of Robert Graves, Dr. Marija Gimbutas, Merlin Stone, Naomi Goldenberg and many others. It presents the externalization of insights gained from those authors, fortified by scholastic and personal studies in biology, psychology, sociology, religion and history, as well as the intellectual strengths bestowed on Athenadorus by his upbringing.

The Danaa is in three sections, each of which starts with an introductory verse. The 'α' section contains three subsections of free verse. This first subsection may also be described as consisting of three parts: (1) the '*Description of Athenadorus*' couched in terms drawn mainly from pre-Indo-european Hellenic and Celtic mythology; (2) Danaan cosmological mythology from the Birth of the Universe through the foundation of Athens; (3) the Danaan Diaspora & Restoration. The 'β' subsection is the mythic restatement of *Tristan and Isolde*; the 'γ' subsection is a myth retelling the plot of Beethoven' *Fidelio*.

The middle section of *The Danaa* is prefaced by two succinct statements of belief, followed by 21 prose sections detailing Athenadorus's philosophy and thealogy. Large parts of what these include are drawn from the natural and social sciences, from economics and history. They detail the rational, science-based view which Athenadorus espouses.

Among the many points put forth in this section are the fact that the female is the original sex; that there is an evolutionary benefit inherent in homosexuality; that the Universe is both subject and source of *laws* which in turn cannot be subject to supernatural disruption or pointillistic revision.

The final section of *The Danaa* is an alphabetical list of the names by which the Goddess has been known and invoked throughout history. No information other than name is given, as this section is intended as a departure point for the reader's further study.

The Phædran Letters are a logical continuation of the middle section of *The Danaa*. These letters start by defining more of the Universe in Danaan terms, and progress further into historical, personal and mythic realms of the Danaan Expansion of self and its realization.

Of principle interest in *The Phædran Letters* is the statement of the central tenet of Danaan philosophy, **The Prime Imperative**, and its associated *Thirteen Freedoms of the Danaans*.

The ***Ta Men Tao*** (the *t*'s are pronounced as *d*'s) is a body of 81 poems which Athenadorus freely rewrote from the Chinese original, the *Tao Te Ching*. The *Ta Men Tao* is not meant to be a pro-forma scholarly translation of the original Taoist document. Athenadorus has taken the original from its bipolar, sexist form and made it more true to the Danaan ideals the *Tao Te Ching* held deeply within itself. This is the only work which has its own introduction, which gives the details of the origin of the *Tao Te Ching* and of Athenadorus's expansive rewriting it.

The general trend within the three works goes from a general mythic, cosmological exposition (*The Danaa*) through the unveiling of ethical, scientific and philosophical vistas (*The Danaa* and *The Phædran Letters*) to a presentation of social and personal insights (the *Ta Men Tao*).

May the *Library* be your *Pegasus*, carrying your spirit on powerful wings to higher planes of personal growth, freedom and tranquility.

Athenadorus
Ἀθηνάδωρος

SUGGESTED READING ORDER
FOR THE FIRST-TIME READER

Because many people are not fully acquainted with ancient (pre-Indo-european and Hellenic) mythology, nor with contemporary works that deal with these and other topics, we present here an order of reading which should allow the reader new to this type of material to follow a path more accessible than the one they would find by trying to read directly through the volume.

The *Ta Men Tao* will, most likely, be the most readily grasped of the various parts of the work. So, that is the suggested starting point:

1. *Ta Men Tao*: Nº 28
2. *Ta Men Tao*: Nº 14
3. *Ta Men Tao*: Introduction, The Prime Imperative & The Thirteen Freedoms
4. *Ta Men Tao*: Nºs 1 - 13
5. *The Danaa*: 1, 3, 9 poems & Sections I - XXI
6. *The Phædran Letters*: Preface
7. *The Phædran Letters*: First & Second Letters
8. *The Danaa*: the first, poetic Division
9. *The Phædran Letters*: Third Letter

During perusal of these portions, one may include further sections from the Tao as the reader may desire.

THE
DANAA

ἈΘΗΝΑΙΗΣ

Λαοῖσι
Ἀθηναδώρου
Βιβλίον Νικολέοιο

THE
DANAA

The·Book·of·the·Nikoleos
Athenadorus
to·the·People·of

ATHENA

Danaan Press

The Greek of the title page is in the Homeric dialect.

EY 5.3005 - 5.3039

THE DANAA: Copyright © 1983, 1996, 2008, 2017 CE by Eduard J. Qualls. All rights reserved. No part of the contents of this book may be reproduced or transmitted in any form or by any means without the express written permission of the publisher.

Ēdidit diē EY 5.3039.VII.03

ἧος ὃ ταῦθ' ὥρμαινε κατὰ φρένα καὶ κατὰ θυμόν,
ἕλκετο δ' ἐκ κολεοῖο μέγα ξίφος, ἦλθε δ' Ἀθήνη
οὐρανόθεν...
στῆ δ' ὄπιθεν, ξανθῆς δὲ κόμης ἕλε Πηλείωνα...
θάμβησεν δ' Ἀχιλεύς, μετὰ δ' ἐτράπετ', αὐτίκα δ' ἔγνω
Παλλάδ' Ἀθηναίην· δεινὼ δέ οἱ ὄσσε φάανθεν

Homer: The Iliad
Book 1, from lines 193-200

while he pondered these two courses in his mind and spirit,
and was pulling the great sword from its sheath, Athena descended
from the sky...
standing at his back, She seized the fair hair of the son of Peleus...
Achilles was startled and turning 'round, recognized immediately
Pallas Athena: her wondrous eyes shining

Translation: Athenadorus

1

I've seen the lone star shining
in the depths of cosmic night
when one world occults all others
and fear gives way to sight

α

In the City of the Crescent
She came to me–most radiant Being
Highest Ruler of the Universe,
On the brightest of nights–unending light
From sun to sun of endless day:
Soft dove coos did banish sleep.
Her Voice calls–the purest Joy!

Child of Life, arise and sing
The Song of Life's Beginning.
Sing of Me, Creator of All,
ATHENA VICTORIOUS, *Greatest and Best.*
Your name I give, my Child, my Love,
Athenadorus Heracles.
Your weapons I give you, three to wield:
The Golden Sword of the more Golden Word,
The Silver Lance of far-reaching Knowledge,
The Ægis Shield of my Devotion.
You are the Messenger, Sacrosanct, of
Renewal, Protection and Liberation.
Persona, Gens, Sapientia:
These are the Three that now shall rule.
You are their Love, my Love, my Child:
I am the One, the Three, the Nine:
This day have I begotten you.
Arise and sing this brightest of Nights
The Mother of the longest of Days.
Sing the Birth of the Universe,
The Feast of Bread, the Feast of Life.
Sing the Birth of Civilization,

Of Farming and Laws and Written Words:
Gifts of the Goddess, from Woman's Hand.
Sing the Orchards heavy with fruit,
The sparkling Waters dark with fish.
Sing the Daughter, Mother and Dame,
Birth, Life and Death, the Three,
Who now do rule, who ruled
And reign.

Gift of Athena, Glory of Hera,
Born of holy Hawthorn moon:
Third child given Life by the Sixth
Of the Company of Nine Sisters,
You have I called to the new-Cephisian
Crescent City of the Tri-lake Hills.
Here is my Home—the seat of Wisdom,
Newly founded in Liberty's Land.
Lay the Foundation and establish my House.
Carry my ancient Message forth to
All my searching, dis-spirited People:
My Sisters will maintain my Home
And, newly free, lead my People in to Me.
Carry my Words and Deeds, my Child, the Words
Of Truth and Hope and Justice.

You are both king and tanist,
    Robin and wren,
        Winter fish and summer serpent.
Within you are the Twins made One,
    You, Virgin born,
    Child of the Moon,
    Of the Virgin reborn,
    Lion of Victory,
    Messenger of Hope,
    Of Freedom new-enfranchised.

Carry my Light of Liberty
*   To the Victims of Oppression's Rule.*
Carry the Love of
*   The Mother long-forgotten,*
*   The Sister long-denied,*
*   The Grandmother too-long neglected.*
You are the charging Lion who scatters
*   The Tyranny of weak-minded Sheep.*
You swing my Sword and shatter the Invaders:
*   The Bug, the Bull and the Skull.*
You ride the four Seas to the endless Horizon
*   To shine the Light of Truth*
*   On this falsehood-sickened World.*

Through forty-six hundred million years
And yet fifty-three thousand more have I
This warm, soft-glistening Earth protected–
From its Birth till even now and forever
Till Time collapse in my Hand, will I
Her creatures cherish. Arise, my Child!
From the waters I arose and sang
The Song of Life Beginning.
The Words fell sweet as gentle spring rain
To nourish a thirsty World:

All was One. All was at Rest.
All was in Unity with the Goddess,
Mother of All Things is She, ATHENA,
Dea Polyonoma, Athena Alexandra,
Grey-eyed Goddess, only Source of Wisdom.
She clapped Her Hands and from the Unity flowed forth
The Trinity of the Universe.
In swirling clouds they played,
Rushing through timelessness, the Three who are the One:
Matter, Process, Energy: the Three that are Life,

Persephone, Demeter, Hera: Waxing, Full, Waning:
Virgin, Mother, Grandmother. The One who is Life.
One omnipotence, unchangeable, forever changing.
Into the vacuum the Universe rushed:
Particles, galaxies, all that exists.
Starmother was born and from Her triune brightness issued
All elements of matter, all forms and shapes that are.
But One, Oh Gift of Gifts, She gave, Her Daughter:
Sweet Lifemother, Gift of Heaven, Protector of Earth,
Source, Maintenance, Agent: Cool Oasismother,
Unique among all minutia, yet still Triune.
You alone, Aquaria, do our little sisters and brothers worship,
Singing to You as they dance before our bows.

Third of the Nine, cosmic Children of Brightness, just one
Small planet in a modest star system, a tiny portion of
The Goddess's Great Creation, yet ATHENA did bless her
    with water pure,
To cool the land, bring forth all forms of Life.
Bright silver Moon She set in course, Guardian and Sister of
The Earth: who pulls the waters round her charge, tides washing
Birthplaces of Life itself.

On Terra's surface, Life beginning grew yet ever abundant,
Creatures great and small, immobile and mobile,
Adaptive and static, all shared the light of the Sun and
The night of the Moon. Triple cycles instituted
    at Time's beginning,
Continued and waxed and waned o'er the Earth. And the
Living things She held so close learned to change, to
Stay, survive. One creature, though, more than all the
    rest was
By the Virgin Mother blest, for it had learned to stand
Upright and raise its hands, free, towards the skies,
To praise ATHENA, Bestower of Life.

From the midst of old Pangæa, the plains
Of grassy Africa, we first stood on
Our own two feet and reached in wonder
Toward the skies.
There did She first come to us,
ATHENA, Goddess, Greatest and Best.
She taught us the art of thought, speech and work,
And gave us tools for our vital protection.
Three human tribes She created: each a special gift
She gave to show Her tenderest Devotion:
Our skin She colored to make us Her Own,
Each tribe a different aspect of
Her divine Emanations.
To each tribe She gave a special Home,
A land for their origination:
The white She guided to Mediterranean shores
And cold, dark forests beyond.
The red She led to the Asian view
Out onto the broad Pacific.
The black She gave the breadth of the
Ancient, game-rich plains; guardians of the
Birthplace She designated them:
Protectors of the Forest.

In the valleys of the Rivers' flow,
The talents most precious ever given by the Goddess,
We received from Her, our Mother, our Life:
Hunger was banished, old age revived
With the marvelous Gift, the Farming of Food.
Cities then grew on the wide Rivers' sides,
With tall, shining temples of the Goddess of Love:
To Her Priestess She gave the Written Word,
For Commerce, Letters, Contracts and Laws;
The records of state: decreed by the senate,

Instruments of Wisdom, the Goddess's Will.
Our Cities flourished, our Riches grew,
All through the Crescent was Humanity renewed.

    Destroyers, tyrants, warriors from the mountainous North descended upon the Peace of the Cities of the Great Mother. The destruction was too great for our eyes. The bringers of writing, law, plenty, of the Art of Civilization, overrun by those who know only slaughter and war. We had ruled ourselves; a community of individuals, life as we wanted it, freedom to be our best for the Goddess and for ourselves. They have brought their oppression; with their mountain phantoms they try to abuse our Mother.

People of Danu, of ATHENA, arise
And sing the story of the skies,
Of knowledge won through struggle.
Renew the journey to Freedom's gate:
To the radiant House of the Goddess.

We left our homes on Tritonis's shore to
Find new fields to plant with crops.
Along the salt sea waves we went, to
Egypt's swelling stream, thence north
Along the Sea's east edge and round again,
But toward the west, toward the setting Moon.
There rest we found, but not for long, for
At our heels barked the mountain men,
Warriors, merciless robber-bands.
From our island, known as Rhodes, into a
Fertile land we trekked, carrying the image
Of our Goddess, until we reached a gentle plain.
There we built our state anew and called it

Pelasgian Argos–the Virgin's loving people,
A new-found home, and rest, at last.
Our cousin clans soon again we found
In the Balkans, in the East and on the Isle of Crete.

When we had grown beyond the Plain,
The Goddess led our clans again to
Search for new horizons.
Through the Isthmus went our path until
The hill, our home we sought, was seen,
Majestic above the Cephisian Plain.
Upon the height in radiant light
She beckoned us forward with voice of might:
Come, People, come! This land awaits
Its ever-growing glory that you bring.
My Joy in this place all will know–
Most Glorious of Cities: its tale will be told
In all nations and in all lands where
Freedom is cherished and Wisdom is dear.
My Name shall it bear: my visage clear
Shall beam a beacon across the strands
To the lovers of Liberty in every land.

  Wielders of the iron sword swung down with their destruction and misery once more. The darkness of the ages was terrible. Learning vanished from among their nations. Only where remnants of our people held fast did civilization survive. Half clung to Aegean shores: all others had to flee.

Out from Hellas west and north went our cousin clans,
Seeking lands where life could be spent
In joy and freedom from vampiric iron.
To Tuscan fields they journeyed,
across the dark Tyrrhenian waves.

And in the north between the seas
Established the marks of Danu's reign.
In the west at Ocean's door they discovered more
Of the land they sought on Iberian plains.
Farther trekked our clans across Gaul until
The Isles' emerald chalk shores we reached
With joy and jubilation: Home were we then
Till whenever again, the Goddess lead us on.

Years and years and years and tears
Have flowed through our lives since
Wooden-walled Athens we last saw:
Driven away, out of our lands, we who
First caressed the seven-hilled Tiber,
Driven out by the accursèd
Tyranny of the dying god and his
Father, mad thunder-slinging fool,
Whose cruel, sword-made, sordid rule
Cost us our land, our liberty, our Life
Of community and love of knowledge.
Only when it suits their cause–
Attempted revivifying of their god–
Will they a truth acknowledge.
Their arsenal of weapons they carry about
And thump before our face: an authorization of
Hatred, genocide, eternal damnation:
The legacy of a godkin who created their world–
An eternal lord–invented only two millennia ago!

We have cried Enough! Enough!
End this growing desolation!
Yet kept he his foot upon our neck, this brother
Preoccupied with death and his god of annihilation.
Now is the sword in our long-captive hands!

Now is the freedom of the Goddess among us!
The freedom of the rule of Law!
Justice and Responsibility.

The clarion call soars o'er the hills
And fills the valleys with all-enrapturing joy
Of Her Eternal Radiance:
She urges us on with mighty song
To Her warm Embrace–to the Mother of All.

Many lands now hold our cousins dear.
But still one city stands most proud and clearly
Warrants our purest affection.
Through centuries of days She has shown the Way,
The Truth of the Love of the Goddess.
Hail! ATHENA, GREATEST AND BEST!
Our Mother, our Protector,
Queen of Athens, City most Blest!

Alles Vergängliche	All that is transient
Ist nur ein Gleichnis;	Is but reflection;
Das Unzulängliche,	All that's inadequate,
Hier wird's Ereignis;	Here becomes perfection;
Das Unbeschreibliche,	The indescribable,
Hier ist's getan;	Here is accomplished;
Das Ewig-Weibliche	The Eternal-Female
Zieht uns hinan.	Leads us here on.

　　　　–Goethe

β

I, a servant of the king, was ordered to
fetch for him his bride.
Mindless, I obeyed.
Onto a ship I escorted Her,
Proud Lady, Priestess, Prize of War.
There at sea Her powers grew–
She opened my two eyes to see
The perfect peace Her Freedom brings.
Then did I learn to love.
The king forced the Lady to be his wife.
(Too-often name of misery and strife.)
My devotion to the Lady grew, until one dawn,
I fought to save my Love from shame,
From repeated submission to the tyrant's gaze.
My longsword sliced false phantoms twice;
Two of the three felled within the sight of
The false king's desperation.
A viral sword gave me my wound:
Poisoned, I sought the Willow's shade
On Her island in the white sea surf.
Over the water, silent I fell–
Beneath the myrtles She came to me.
On a birch bed cool in willow's shades,
A fig she placed on my lips: I died
Held tight in the Virgin's embrace.
Now as She sings, I swim joyously through
The surging waves of warm caresses
Of Athena's unending Love.
She sings to me, Her porpoise-son.
She garlands me with oak and elder
And feeds me with the figs of Life
In the waters of blue Eternity:
The king is banished, the tyrant's destroyed:
Again She rules, the Goddess rules:
Sweet Liberty, Sweet Justice,
Great Queen!

γ

I am imprisoned in a dark, damp dungeon of fear and misery. I have dared to speak the Truth, to wonder at the Universe, and to question the history and meaning of Life. He came in the cold midwinter, blindfolded me and gagged me: I could think, hear, read, say and do only that which his decrees allowed. Imprisoned, I sat, chilled, thirsty, hungry. Few were the meager crusts his agent brought and dumped in the empty manger.

Down he comes into my cell, to murder me for striving against fallacy and his ministers of falsehood, to imprison me eternally in the irretrievable depths of the Earth.

Light and warmth, a woman's voice:

Redemption, Joy without peer, Freedom, Peace, an end to fear, and blessed, blessed, blessed Truth stream from Your Form

O Goddess, of all things most Beautiful,
Sweet Fountain of Life,
Most Tender Love.

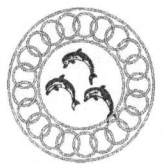

3

When over the forest the moon sits low
With face so bright, like virgin snow,
I feel the pull of unearthly power
That makes strong men weep
And heroes cower

Her voice calls, simply, sweetly, pure:
Come to Me now, this lamp is your
One guide to the Knowledge
Of all that is and was and
Ever shall be—the path is yours—
Your task—to seek

VNAM·COLIMVS·DEAM

WE WORSHIP ONE GODDESS, Eternal, Unchangeable, Always Changing:
  Creator of all Universes: Source of Life, *She is Life itself.*
    She is the One Named of Many Names:
    She is ATHENA.
We worship Her in Her Trinity: *Virgin, Mother, Grandmother*:
    ATHENA *Artemis*, ATHENA *Demeter*, ATHENA *Hera*.
We worship Her in Her Lunar Trinity: *waxing, full, waning*: black, white, red:
    She is the Phases of the Moon–the Faces of Humanity.
    She is the Trinity of Existence: *matter, transformation, energy.*
    She is the Unifying Force: *creating, transforming, destroying.*
We worship Her in Her Nonity: *Her Unity of Nine*:
  She is the Muses–*the Spirit of Civilization.*
    She is Wisdom, Contentment and Peace.
    She is Love.
All supernatural power is ATHENA.
All international power is ATHENA.
All intranatural power is ATHENA.

THE GODDESS Is the first deity worshiped by humanity. She has been worshiped without ceasing for over fifty-thousand years.

She creates the Universe in Her Unity, nurtures it through Her Trinity, preserves it through Her Nonity: Her Unity of Nine.
She is the Life of the Universe, and reveals Herself in the triune basis of that Life: matter, transformation, energy — gas, liquid, solid — past, present, future.

She is the Moon, watchful Guardian, Teacher of Humanity, her Phases being three: waxing, full, waning. Such also are the stations of all Creatures: Birth, Life and Death. The Phases of the Moon reveal the three Faces of humanity: black, red, white. In the Unity of these are we consecrated to Her.

She leads our path through Life: Virgin, Mother, Grandmother. Thus Goethe called Her: *Virgin, Mother, our Chosen Queen.*

She is invoked with many names, but Her Name of greatest Love and Honor is ATHENA. Her people worship Her in calling themselves by another very ancient Name of Hers: *Danaans*, the People of Danu, who is ATHENA.

I.

The Universe and all it contains are one substance, continuous in all dimensions, complete unto itself and comprehensible to the mind of the human animal.

All forms of energy, transformation and matter act consistently, in ways totally uniform with the nature of the Universe itself: for even randomness is ordered according to the structure of the Universe.

As human mental abilities have evolved and continue to develop, we have begun cataloguing these qualities of consistency in what we call Natural Law.

This ability to derive rational understanding from the seemingly irrational is a characteristic unique to Humanity. For, although almost all animals are capable of superstitious behavior, only humankind is able to go beyond superstition to a sane, logical and clear exposition of the Truth which is the Universe.

The Space-Time Continuum is the web woven of the intersections of the continua of all dimensions. Natural Law is the explication of the identities and interrelationships which exist among these dimensional continua. Matter and energy are warps in the Space-Time Continuum; transformation is the relationship between these warps and between those warps and the Space-Time Continuum itself.

One important law of the Universe is that, given a certain condition in a certain time span, all outcomes are determined by the nature of the Space-Time Continuum itself: no other results are at all possible in this Universe.

II.

Each entity or concept is a system.

A system consists of three elements: inputs, process and outputs. This is yet another manifestation of the Trinity of the Universe.

Biologically, the three elements are seen, for example, in the respiratory system: the inputs are waste-laden blood, fresh air and the physical construction of the lungs; the process is the exchange of gases between air and blood; the outputs are refreshed blood, less-fresh air and the lungs, ready again to undertake the process whenever further inputs are made available by other systems. In the social realm, the three elements are easily seen in such activities as business, in health care and in government.

Concepts have as inputs human experience with the concept; as process, the concept's manifestation and use in current human experience; and as outputs, the concept's reshaping effects on human experience.

III.

Each thing that exists is a system that is connected to those things around it: that is, it has inputs and outputs by which it is in some way linked to other systems, and to its own appropriate supersystems and subsystems. A system may have any number of supersystems to which it belongs, and any number of subsystems which belong to it.

IV.

A *law* is the reduction to human symbols of a systems interface process between two entities or concepts that exist in this Universe.

A law is a system in and of itself.

V.

The origin of life as we know it was an occurrence of importance, magnitude and wonder, second only to the origin of the Universe itself. It is essential to the further development of the human species that we understand the nature of this event, that we realize the truth of the occasion so that we may turn from superstition, guilt and fear, to progress along the path of enlightenment.

The birth of Life was no accident. It was not the effect of random happenstance. It was not the product of some godling's bending uncooperative substance into form. Life came into being because, given the nature of the Universe, it was the only result possible. The start of Life does not require supernatural intervention, or the hand of a "maker". For, this occurrence was not like someone's throwing a handful of iron ore into the air and having an assembled watch fall to the ground. Rather, it was like the melting of snow on a warming winter's day: given the nature of the Universe and the structure of the physical world, that is what in all like circumstances, in any epoch **must** happen.

For Life not to have begun–*that* would have been the true miracle. It would have necessitated turning the Universe "upside-down," or at least the deletion of certain elements from the Periodic Table, most importantly nitrogen.

As a concept, Life is difficult to define. It has different meanings in different cultures. Something considered dead, or lifeless, in one society may be considered fully alive in another. Yet a viable definition is not only possible, it is necessary.

That is alive which is an entity capable of purposeful interaction: capable of both self-duplication and synthesis.

Amino acids, the basic building blocks of all proteins (and, therefore, of all terrestrial Life), are abundant in this Universe. In the primordial puddles of the young Earth the chemicals and conditions were present which allowed for these plentiful amino acids to form into the long chains which characterize proteins. In the succeeding course of events, which were as technically complicated as the evaporation of a pool of water in the mid-day sun, these myriad proteins formed spheres–protocells–which, merely because of the physical nature of the protein molecules of which they were composed, were capable of replication and synthesis. Indeed, these seemingly simple spheres of proteins were alive, even without the presence of a nucleic acid memory-bank, and without any mythical, supernatural intercession. Their replication was effected through absorption and construction–colonization on a molecular level. If at least one of each of the vital proteins of the parent protocell was available to the daughter cell, more copies of it could in turn be constructed by drawing on the contents of the surrounding aqueous solution, using simple osmotic molecular flows, absorbing the proteins produced by the action of the sun's ultraviolet radiation upon the amino acids present in the primordial soup.

DNA does not have to be present for Life to exist. It facilitates its orderly continuation and expedites the evolutionary process, but it is not the precursor or arbiter of Life. Proteins are active without DNA, but DNA is biologically inert without the proteins which manipulate it.

We are alive because the structure of protein molecules creates in them the ability to live. We are alive because Life itself is a quality inherent in the Space-Time Continuum.

Life is the Nature of the Universe.

VI.

Each animal begins its development as an immature female of its species. Its gene structure later instigates those changes which determine its mature physical sexual characteristics. However, since the male never completely loses those female characteristics he began with (*e.g.*, externally: nipples, and internally: remnants of his original vagina and uterus), the male is shown to be an adaptation of the female for the purpose of evolution through genetic variation.

Each human life begins within the femaleness of its mother. The female gives it substance, the male gives it impetus, and between them is Life.

The female is the original form—the default form—of life. The male is an adaptation of that original form, created as a mechanism of sexual reproduction.

In order for a fetus to become a male, two sets of chemical actions must be added to the basic, original female-specific sequence: (1) hormones must first make the fetus stop developing into a female, then (2) different hormones must cause the fetus to develop the physical attributes of maleness.

Despite any encoded genetic directions as to the sex of the embryo, if the appropriate hormones are not introduced, the physical and sexual development of that embryo will be that of a genetic female. Without the introduction of extra chemicals to alter it, the destiny of all fetuses is to be female.

In mammalian females, who have the sex-chromosome structure designated 'XX', only one of the two X-chromosomes is functional; the other X-chromosome shrivels into an inactive clump called a *Barr body*. Therefore, a female is a creature with one X-chromosome.

In male mammals, with the sex-chromosome structure 'XY', there is but one functional X-chromosome, exactly as is true in the female. The presence of the Y-chromosome is simply to provide the mechanisms that create those hormones and their reactions necessary to change a female embryo into a male and then to maintain those sex-based structures and processes throughout the male's existence.

The female is the original. The male is its second form, its second realization, its second incarnation.

There are certain cellular organelles and chemicals which can only be inherited from the female parent, and without which animals and plants could not survive:

1. No cellular or multicellular animal or plant could live if its individual cells did not contain mitochondria. A mitochondrion is much like a refinery, in that it takes certain chemicals absorbed or transported into the cell from the blood or other nutrient medium and transforms those chemicals' energies into forms the other cell organelles can use to power their tasks. Once independent cells, mitochondria have their own DNA, the control of which, along with their reproduction schedule, remains largely independent of the DNA of the cell itself. Mitochondria are not transferred from male parent to offspring: the sperm cell (or pollen grain) is itself too small, and the few mitochondria in the tail of the sperm are destroyed during the process of fertilization. All the millions of mitochondria you have in your body came from your mother and from her mother and so on back through time immemorial to the Original, the Mother of All Living. As with mitochondria in all cells, so too with the chloroplasts in plant cells. Chloroplasts are those organelles that harvest the light of the Sun to power chemical reactions which break down carbon dioxide and water to form compounds called hydrocarbons, the structural components of plant-cell walls and the energy supply of both the plants which produce them and animals which eat the plants. These chloroplasts are organelles that are also inherited only from the female parent.
2. In the first weeks after fertilization, the nuclei in the cells of embryos are so preoccupied with copying and re-copying the chromosomes, to make more and more nuclei, that they have no time to construct the messages and structures (*mRNA*, *tRNA* and *rRNA*) needed to keep the cellular processes functioning. During this time, all the RNA available and all the cellular structures functioning are those which were prepared before fertilization, when the ovum was still a part of the mother's body. During this

period, all cellular processes of the embryo are identical to those of the mother.
3. The primary disease-resistance capacity which protects newborn mammals are complex proteins, immuno-globulins, inherited directly from the mother: infused from her own body-fluids into the body fluids of the embryo. These are later augmented by the immunity-inducing chemicals passed to the child by the mother, in her milk.

The female is the original form of Life. The male is a form derived from that original; a form that provides genetic stimuli which encourage adaptation and development of that Life, as the immediate agent of Evolution.

VII.

On the continuum of sexuality that exists in animal species, we find three points that are the three gender-aspects: the female, termed the *gyneic*; the *laotrophic*; and the male, or *aneric*. This is the Trinity of the Goddess Within. Each entity contains all three gender-aspects to varying degrees; one, however, usually predominates. The following are examples of the general concepts identified with each gender-aspect:

gyneic (*female*):	**laotrophic**:	**aneric** (*male*):
creation	transformation	destruction
synthesis	metakinesis	catalysis
generation	interrelation	dissipation
substance	time	movement
birth	life	death
centripetal	orbital	centrifugal
matter	transformation	energy

In women, the female gender-aspect predominates; in homosexuals, the laotrophic is foremost; in men, the male gender-aspect prevails. In Danaan symbolism these three gender-aspects are mirrored by the Triad: Virgin, Mother, Grandmother: the "growing-of-life", the "giving-of-life", the "fading-of-life".

The gender-aspects are a continuum: the three designations are points of reference, not discrete boxes; nor are they judgments or moral pronouncements. As human beings, we draw from each as we need the qualities inherent in each, realizing that exclusive over-emphasis on any one of them will be detrimental to our mental or physical health, detrimental to our survival as the species at the pinnacle of terrestrial evolution.

VIII.

The most basic system—the basic unit—that forms human society is the individual. The individual belongs to its father's family and to its mother's clan. The family is the aneric, the clan is the gyneic and the individual is the interface between the two.

The clan is the basic operative unit of the Danaans because it provides a more stable building-block for society than does the nuclear family. Because the clan is the extended-family unit, its broader structure allows for more extensive supportive relationships. Society is the great supersystem composed of the interactions between and among individuals, families and clans.

When a child is born, it is given one or two forenames, followed by its father's family name (its *patronym*), followed in turn by its mother's clan name (its *matronym*).

Upon affirming the marriage contract in the celebration of the Conubia, the male replaces his matronym with that of the woman; and the woman replaces her patronym with that of the man. This shows that the man has left the clan of his mother and has been accepted into the clan of the woman. For a woman, taking the man's patronym reveals that she has agreed to enter into a partnership with him, thus allying her clan with his family.

When laotrophics affirm their partnership vows, each adds the other's clan name to the end of their own names. This represents the linking function laotrophics perform in society when they enter into connubial relationships.

IX.

The danger inherent in over-emphasis of any one of the gender-aspects is greatest when it is the aneric gender-aspect that is amplified. Although conditions of over-emphasizing the other two gender-aspects, *gyneic hypertrophy* and *laotrophic endotrophy*, do exist, these are much rarer than over-emphasis of the aneric, and they more often tend to have very narrow fields of effects and lesser impacts.

Individuals do themselves great harm when they allow themselves to slip into a condition of over-emphasis on the aneric, a mental and emotional state called **hyperaneric atrophy**. This most often occurs at times of great emotional, mental or physical stress.

The onset of a state of hyperaneric atrophy is characterized by useless hyperactivity–franticness, worrying, overwrought emotions, manic-depressive swings, the dissipation of energy in non-productive activity: a dog chasing its own tail; a flash flood of nervous energy that accomplishes nothing and can be very destructive.

When one does nothing to alleviate the condition of hyperaneric atrophy, the gyneic core of the individual often will assert itself and will attempt to take action to attempt preservation of the organism: when the problem is mental or emotional, it will cause the neocortex to generate false signals: neuroses or psychoses, which are the gyneic core's warning that something unnoticed or ignored is a threat to the continued existence of that individual.

When the problem produces physical effects, such as accidents or self-inflicted injuries, the gyneic core will shut down the neocortex: whether with sleep, shock or by means of coma depends on the seriousness of the physical shock incurred. When the gyneic core causes increased sleep, it is asserting the body's attempt to heal itself, by diverting blood and nutrition to the site of injury rather than allowing the individual to utilize those resources in wakeful activities. In the case of shock and coma, the gyneic is not functioning to preserve the individual life, but is functioning as the soothing guardian: easing suffering by severing consciousness and the awareness of pain. This is a state labeled *gyneic hypertrophy*.

The consequence of such trauma is, more often, not so outwardly drastic as fully expressed psychoses or coma. The fully developed psyche in a condition of aneric atrophy will start to doubt its abilities to cope, and so will turn away from its own capacities to an external authority figure, in order to give itself some relief from having to deal with its condition, situation and responsibilities: responsibilities both for itself and for its actions. In this way hyperaneric atrophy is the origin of Oedipal complexes, for those external authority figures turned to are substitutes for the individual's adult instincts and capabilities; those external are masters who replace the individual's own internal adult, the gyneic core.

The single greatest symptom of hyperaneric atrophy is the negation of self: lack of self-confidence, self-worth, self-dignity. It is this lack of realization of the self, this ignoring of the gyneic center, that allows others to take over the hyperaneric's mind, life and livelihood. This is the source of the power of the father-god religions.

Hyperaneric atrophy can effect and be prolonged by larger social groups, cities, nations, cultures. The Indo-europeans brought this condition into the civilized world in order to eviscerate the spirit of the peoples they oppressed, and the Earth has suffered from its effects for thousands of years. The systems they instituted provided for the protection of the male, white Indo-european warriors through the bloody subjugation of the Goddess-worshiping peoples, the destruction of the bringers of Civilization. They deprived women of their rights as individuals and lowered them to the status of chattel; to homosexuals they denied all rights of existence; non-whites existed only for the benefit of their white conquerors.

There has been no sparing of Nature since the priests of the father-gods took over. Only the deserts have increased since their father-god assumed his throne: the Sahara, the floor of the

Mediterranean. Worst of all is the desert of the human mind they have engendered and spread.

The Brahmins destroyed the Ganges-dwellers, worshipers of Devi; the Levites slaughtered the Palestinians, the devoted of Anatha; the Dorians burned Aphrodite-engendered Troy; the Goths assaulted Venus-born Rome; Byzantines and Moslems destroyed Isis-born Egypt. The priests of oppression have all strived to keep the worshipers of the Goddess beneath the level of slavery.

The only creation of hyperanerics is war.

Most frustrating to the hyperaneric followers of the father-gods is the fact that true progress occurs only when the People of the Goddess reassert Her Presence: Ancient Egypt and Sumeria, Classical Greece and Rome, 525th to 527th-century France, Elizabethan England, Renaissance France and Italy, Revolutionary America and France, the Age of Goethe in German-speaking countries, post-Civil War America, post-Napoleonic and post-Second Empire France, Victorian and Windsor Britain, the Weimar Republic and post-World War II Germany.

X.

One of the greatest achievements of the People of the Goddess since the establishment of the Athenian democracy is the Constitution of the United States of America, with its prologue, the Declaration of Independence. The Constitution is the Unity composing the Trinity: the Congress, Supreme Court and Presidency are societal counterparts of the Universal Trinity—*matter, transformation, energy*: creation, interpretation, execution: gyneic, laotrophic, aneric.

The United States has withstood several crises of hyperaneric atrophy within the last several decades: the Viet Nam conflict was a creation of the presidents—an action undertaken beyond the constitutional limits of their office. The American involvement was ended only by the combined outcry of those who loved the Constitution more than they did the President. The use of the Central Intelligence Agency as the President's secret army has repeatedly proved disastrous. And then there is the Nixon syndrome: when the aneric over-reaches itself and threatens the safety of the organism, the gyneic will take action to insure the survival of the entity: Congress prevailed.

XI.

There are three auspicious occurrences which instigate the processes that bring about the existence of new life. These three occurrences are (1) fertilization of the egg; (2) the beginning of the functioning of the brain; and (3) birth.

Fertilization is the instant at which the process of *somatoplasis* begins, the molding of the physical body. The functioning of the electronic circuitry of the brain gives the development of the mind, *phrenoplasis*, its start. Birth commences the process called *psychoplasis*, the realization of the soul. These are the three processes that are involved in the gradual separation of a part of the mother-entity into entities of new life.

All three processes continue throughout life, though at varying rates and with changing effects. Somatoplasis has its most visible effects between birth and young adulthood, at which point its effects change from emphasis on growth to emphasizing maintenance. Later, its process guides the physical changes associated with increasing age.

The most remarkable products of phrenoplasis occur in childhood, when the new life begins to grasp the possibilities inherent in its relationship with its environment.

Psychoplasis begins at the moment of physical separation of the child from its mother: the beginning of new life. For a time the new life had been cradled from the outside world, from the Universe, by the soul of its mother–it was nourished as a portion of her own being during the period between onset of phrenoplasis and birth because it did not as yet have a soul of its own.

First it had no body of its own: somatoplasis provides it with a body. Then it had no mind of its own: phrenoplasis satisfies that need. Complete independence was achieved when the new life, in leaving its mother's aura, her field of gravity, her soul, was given its soul, a divine portion of the Goddess Herself.

This gift of a soul, given by Athena to all living things, contains the three gender-aspects that will shape and determine the nature of the life of the new entity. In early childhood, the gyneic asserts itself so that the mind has the time necessary to interconnect itself with the body and the soul, so that all may inter-react, and so that all may consolidate themselves, individually.

XII.

Life as detailed above may be compared to the most common form, or isotope, of hydrogen. The soul is the proton nucleus, the center and stability of the atom; the body is the electron, the external cloud which determines the atom's interactional characteristics, its physical properties; the mind is the energy field interconnecting the other two, guiding the body and providing unity.

In the realm of this allegory, a concept may be properly compared to an atom if it can be understood without needing to be split further into simpler precepts, or if, under scrutiny, it holds together as a conceptual entity.

All relationships, physical and conceptual, are *bibiotic* [*by-by-áh-tic*], that is, they involve two lives: "βι-βίος". More complexity is added when, for example, a group interacts, because several bibiotic relationships are superimposed: indeed, there are fifteen bibiotic relationships among a group of six communicants, and twenty-eight bibiotic relationships among a group of eight.

A bibiotic relationship is, in the terminology of the chemical, atomic metaphor, a covalent bond which forms a molecule of two atoms. The bibiotics share electrons, that is to say, they share physical information when they are in a molecular configuration, in a relationship. They do not link souls, nor do they meld into one entity: each retains its individual integrity, even while involved in a molecular-synergistic interrelationship.

The essential characteristics of a human bibiotic relationship are not pre-set as they are in chemical or mathematical bibiotic relationships. Mathematical relationships are governed by universal law: they are constant, predictable and purely quantifiable. Human bibiotic relationships are contractual in nature, as it is the two entities involved who determine the characteristics of their symbiosis.

XIII.

Humans enter into relationships when the potential of realizing a benefit is perceived to be inherent within the nature, evolution or secondary effects of those relationships. The two humans together produce mutual effects which may be seen as the products, direct or indirect of the relationship.

This close association of two humans in a situation in which the total effect of the association is greater than that of the combined effects of the two as independent agents is termed a *synergistic relationship*: the whole is greater than the sum of its parts.

The benefit realized is a part of that *synergistic product-set* which is the actual synergic aspect of the relationship: that of each of the parties involved and that of the synergistic effect produced by the close association of the two. For these reasons, human contractual relationships are labeled *bibiotic*, i.e., involving two lives, and also *trireic*, which means 'composed of three realities'.

The synergistic product-set contains three subsets: the benefit-set, the neutral-set and the detriment-set. The nature of each of these is determined by the mental, physical and psychical needs of the individual.

Although these factors are most easily discerned in what are termed *love relationships*, they exist and function in all human relationships and, indeed, pervade the animal and plant world.

Before entering into a relationship, each of the parties potentially involved must (1) decide what the product-set of the relationship would be; (2) grasp the relative importance of the benefit-set, neutral-set and detriment-set and their interactions in order to come to some idea as to the most likely outcome (the net-benefit) of the relation; (3) weigh this outcome against his or her own needs, abilities and aspirations. Having reached this point, each party can determine what will be in its best interest, and what will be in the other party's best interest, as well.

The net-benefit is the result of contrasting the benefits of association with the detriments of association. This result can be positive, negative or neutral.

Yet, all relationships exist in time and are therefore subject to the changes which can occur with the passage of time. Because of this, the benefits and detriments perceived as being generated by the relationship must be weighted: benefits received sooner are more valuable than those received later and detriments experienced sooner are more problematical than those that will arise later. In applying this concept of *the change in valuation over time* from finance–"a dollar received today is worth more than a dollar received a year from now"–we arrive at the fully formed term, *the net present-value of relationships*. This net value is the "bottom line" as to whether a relationship is or will be good for each of the two involved.

The processes of evaluation outlined above imply a high level of maturity on the part of those who must decide. They presuppose an ability to deal objectively with personal situations and to think problems through to logical conclusions. They show that each person must know his or her capabilities and growth-patterns. Each must also understand the capacities and traits of the other, the potential partner. Most importantly, they emphasize the tremendous need for self-knowledge that exists in human life.

One of the most important variables in this process of decision-making is the level of uncertainty against which the participants must work. Before, as well as during the relationship, the greater the level of uncertainty, the greater the likelihood of failure. The greatest danger from uncertainty comes from the uncertainty in establishing how the synergistic net-benefit compares with the net-benefit of each as an individual. Any lack of maturity or self-knowledge (which are, after all, the same) increases the amount of uncertainty that is built into the decision.

Uncertainty may arise from change in one or both of the partners; from change in the environment in which the relationship must function; or from the effects of the uncertainty which has been built into the nature of the relationship itself.

Synergistic relationships fail when the net-benefit derived by one of the two, as an individual, surpasses the net-benefit received from the synergy of the relationship. The individual, at that point, would tend to withdraw from the now unprofitable contractual arrangement, unless there were other, overriding reasons for attempted continuation. This constrained continuation, however, will lead to emotional problems and, very likely, to physical symptoms as well. If left unresolved, this state of mind will progress into hyperaneric atrophy and deepening emotional and physical distress.

XIV.

Because of the nature of our interactive capability, we are limited to dealing with others in one of three ways. When interacting with one person, we treat that person singly. When interacting with two people, we either treat them as a single communicative-grouping and establish a single communication link, or we treat them as two individuals, establishing separate communication links with each, then alternate the interactive channel from one to the other. We may also identify strongly with a group to which we belong or to which we feel close ties and thus, may interact as if we were a group, with individuals or with other groups.

The following interactive combinations are therefore possible:

        individual ↔ individual
        individual ↔ group
        group ↔ group

One line of interaction is established between each interactant. An interactant may be either an individual or a group. Many lines of communication may exist when one is dealing with a larger group, at which time these lines of interaction are layered by each involved in accordance with the importance of the communication itself, of the communication-link, or of the communicator, as perceived by that interactant.

The three roles which one may occupy in an interactive situation, either as 'active' sender of the message or as 'active' or 'passive' receiver of the message, are (1) that of *prime-interactant*: the one individual or group who exert a communicative attempt; (2) that of *subinteractant*: an individual who is the receptor of the proffered communication; or (3) that of *caulinteractant*: a member of the group toward which the message has been directed. The main difference between each of these is the level of energy expended in trying to communicate. The energy level decreases as one goes from speaker to enthusiastic listener to a casual listener, for example.

The prime-interactant is described as an individual or a group because a group expressing a message will try to put forward as singular a point of reference and attention as possible, and therefore will rely on a single exponent, a single unifying image, to represent itself, using, as much as possible, an approach stressing unanimity.

A subinteractant is an individual actively receiving the message generated by a prime-interactant. A caulinteractant is a more passive receiver, usually part of a group of people, toward whom the message is directed, but not necessarily *targeted*. A caulinteractant often seems as attentive as a cabbage-plant (Latin *caulis*).

The skill of an orator can well be gauged in her or his ability to convince caulinteractants to elevate their state to that of subinteractant. It may be said from this that a great orator does not go directly into communication, but leads the audience through *communification* into communication.

The way in which a group will relate, both to itself and to its constituent members, will be one of these three:
(1) a **sinecratic** relationship in which there is no over-reaching or all-encompassing synthesis, as in mob-rule or anarchy;
(2) an **intracratic** relationship in which the members of the group aspire to establish their own rules of interrelationship by mutual assent, as is the way in democracies; or
(3) an **extracratic** situation in which control of all relationships, internal and external to the group, are determined by individuals external to the group. This last arrangement describes such conditions as one-person or one-party dictatorships, oligarchies, autocratic principalities and theocracies.

XV.

The concept of sin-and-punishment, of *morality*, has no place in a rational, non-superstitious life. Such arbitrary notions are tools of those who would control other people's lives: for good and evil are concepts which do not exist in Nature.

This simplistic moral division, this imperial bipolar-ism of good and evil is an artifact of the hyper-aneric atrophy forced on the world by the warriors and priests of Jove/Jahveh. A device created by them to extend and perpetuate their control over the people they conquered, it is still the basic mind-control method used by the father-god religions, a dichotomy which they have spread throughout all their theology, philosophy and liturgy: good against evil, white against black, male against female, heterosexual against homosexual, the West against the East, the North against the South, heaven against hell, young against old, us against them, me against you.

Such **pointillistic extremism** is divisive in emphasizing the most remote possibilities, in making either/or situations; in creating ravaging self-righteousness and isolationism; and in denying the interrelationships of all things, all people, all times, in trying to cut into tiny pieces the fabric of the interwoven Universe. It is the root of **paranoid schizophrenia** on a global scale.

Sin is a disease invented by those who wanted to rule the lives of others by controlling dispersal of the "cure".

By declaring that "all (others) have sinned," these fabricators put forth the fiction that, as they alone have received knowledge of the definition of "sin"—and of the difference between sin and non-sin—they alone are the "chosen" ones, the ones designated by the gods of their manufacture to judge you, and to dispense the "prescription" to make you "whole" again–a cure for sale at the tremendous price, though, of their seizing control over your very life. Cure, indeed!

All creatures are guided in their behavior by the three clauses of their Contract of Life, by the Prime Imperative: they need no revelation from on-high, no memos from a high-priest's psychosis, no superstitious berating and bewailing.

Good and evil do not exist in Nature. Natural elements and forces are neither 'good' nor 'evil': they simply exist.

The actions of creatures living in a pure state of nature are a delicate balance among three powerful drives: that for survival of the individual, for survival of the kinship or identity group and for survival of the species. These drives are the three clauses of each creature's Contract of Life–the Three Imperatives within the Prime Imperative. This creature's life consists of that behavior which is in agreement with the individual's Contract of Life: its Natural Contract that it will live its life in such a way so as to maximize the survival chances of Life itself.

Humans commit acts of violence against themselves and others because they have lost the ability to keep their lives in balance, because they have failed to nurture a state of equilibrium among the Three Imperatives. Most acts of violence are rooted in a misguided over-emphasis on self, to the detriment of the other two drives.

The three gender-aspects are genetically based reinforcements of the three contractual clauses, a societal broadening of the attempt to establish that balance among self, family/identity-group and species. The male, aneric gender-aspect is individual-oriented; the homosexual, laotrophic gender-aspect is culture- and society-oriented; the female, gyneic gender-aspect is species-oriented.

The male is an animal of self, of the individual: the male guards *his* territory, *his* group of females, and so on. It is because of attitudes generated within the human individual, in society or from aspects of genetics that his behavior is modified so as to be altruistic.

The female is, by biological design, the key to the survival of the species. It is she who carries within her, from birth, the eggs that will be all future generations.

Homosexuality is a genetic biological response to the need for greater gathering and concentration of resources for the use of family- or identity-groups. Homosexuality occurs with statistical regularity in all mammal species and is the primary gender-aspect of approximately 10% of the human species.

The way in which these laotrophics contribute to the survival of their groups is easily discernible upon closer inspection of history. In ancient societies–Egypt, Sumer, Greece, Rome and Native America–homosexuals were vital members of their tribes, clans and communities. By not producing offspring, while at the same time remaining within their kinship groups, the strengths and abilities of these homosexual tribal members went into helping their parents, their grandparents, their siblings and those siblings' children survive. They increased the tribe's food-production and self-protection capacities without increasing the load on the clan's survivability.

In Western civilization, this nourishment augmentation has shown itself in cultural areas, where homosexuals have harvested the spirit of their societies, distilled it and re-presented it in intensely concentrated and revealing forms. One need only hear some of the names – da Vinci, Michelangelo, Marlowe, Shakespeare, Handel, Beethoven, Hilda Doolittle and Stein, not to mention the Ancients, such as Sappho, Archilochus, Solon and Socrates – to understand the reinforcing effects this genetic capacity has had for Civilization.

Maintained in equilibrium and allowed to work together in the proportions established by natural selection, the three gender-aspects provide a strong biological guide, a basis for the survival of our species and of terrestrial Life itself.

XVI.

Upon the birth of a child, the parents of that child enter into a contract with the newborn, in which the Goddess grants the parents the joy, love and bright dreams that the infant brings, and they assume the responsibility of caring for another living being needful of instruction, protection and tender guidance. The infant never 'belongs' to its parents: they are custodians blest with a task of love, acting vicariously for the Goddess Herself.

The parents assume certain responsibilities for the dependent infant during its formative years. Later, the infant will assume those deferred responsibilities for its parents when their advancing years invite similar dependencies.

XVII.

The soul is the Goddess Within.

Athena donates the soul, a portion of Her Self, as a result of the Contract of Life between Her and that entity.

The entity achieves Life, a benefit, and incurs for this consideration responsibilities which provide consideration in return. These responsibilities we have as living creatures are (1) to protect and nourish the Goddess's People; (2) to continue, cultivate and improve those early gifts of the Goddess, the gifts which brought about the birth of Civilization; and (3) to search after knowledge of one's self, one's surroundings, and the Universe: that is to say, to search for knowledge of **ATHENA**, Great Goddess, Spirit of Existence, Mother of All Living.

XVIII.

There is an attitude toward oneself, toward those creatures with whom we share this Earth, and toward the Contract of Life we each have made with the Goddess, which will permit us the greatest opportunities for personal growth, personal contentment and peace, and will most benefit our fellow creatures. This attitude is called *pietas*.

Someone whose life exhibits pietas is someone who is living at one with the Universe, at one with the Goddess, is someone who knows the true, all-pervading joy of Her Liberation.

Each freedom carries with it much responsibility. A large part of the ability to enjoy and preserve freedom springs from the capacity to recognize, deal with and execute those responsibilities. Pietas is the realization and uncomplaining performance of these duties.

Knowledge is sacred.

Love of knowledge is love of the Goddess.

Questioning, searching, striving after knowledge is one of the greatest acts of the human animal. It is a pinnacle of pietas.

Thirst for the truth is a longing for the Goddess. Wisdom is Her Gift allowing satisfaction of that thirst.

Respect for oneself and for one's infinite capacity for love and compassion is the beginning of the realization of pietas. From this grows respect for others and a true desire to understand and share the life-forces at work within oneself, with others and throughout the world. From this grows the realization of the Greater Self–the individual as part of the Self of the Universe–the Self which is the Goddess.

Pietas is Respect.
Pietas is Love.
Pietas is Wisdom.
Pietas is Oneness with the Goddess.

XIX.

Death is the cessation of the transformation between matter and energy. In the physical body, this is manifested in the ending of neural activity. This lack of electrical energy causes the mind to evaporate, which liberates the body to rejoin the Earth and frees the soul to return to the Goddess.

XX.

At death the soul is assayed by the Trinity of Infinite Reunion to ascertain whether this soul has fulfilled its Contract of Life.

⸙ If it has violated it utterly, it will be re-dissolved into gravity and its waves will be scattered unreunitable among the galaxies.

⸙ If it has barely approached fulfilling its contract and has done little or nothing to help itself or to further society, it will be reborn as a human, so that it will have a chance to try again to reach toward the Goddess, to be more than merely a survivor.

⸕ Those who go beyond their contract in striving for the betterment of themselves and for the betterment of the condition of life of their fellow creatures, who reach out to find greater knowledge of the Universe and all it contains, who strive to be One with the Goddess, shall attain Unity with Her: immortal porpoise-children, souls happy and free, swimming in the warmth of Her all-encompassing Love, far beyond the time-horizon of the Universe. These Blessed, these Divine Ones may be reincarnated to aid humanity when and where they are most needed, in times of humanity's distress.

XXI.

We are a people of Life, a people of the Earth, a people of the wide Universe.

We are a people of Love: love of our physical existence, love of Nature, love of the Goddess.

We are a people of Knowledge and of the striving for that knowledge. We are a questioning, searching, discovering people.

We are the Transcendents: unbound by the limits of space or time. We are the Adults of the Goddess.

WE ARE THE PEOPLE OF ATHENA.

9

When we stood in the dust
Of Tranquility Base;
And gave witness to the Earth,
Rising gentle above grey lunar mounts,
Far-distant Earth, in the Sea of Night,
Warm brown, shimmering blue and bright–
Caressed in cloud-swept majesty,
Then were we reborn–delivered–
Unto greater realms
Of understanding

When our hands gave us gift of wondrous sight
Of the Sun's dying rays in the Martian night,
Of lightning's flash in Jupiter's bands,
Of the crystalline rings, great Saturn's clan of
Ice, and rocky amateurs,
Then did She more fully unveil Herself
To our exspectant glances–progress–
Through our own
Endeavor

In our searching
She gives of Herself.
Through our questions,
She reveals Herself.
For our inner growth
Her joy resounds–
Universal Love, immense, unbound

ONOMACRENEIA

This Onomacreneia, this *Fountain of Names of the Goddess*, is a continually growing list of a few of the vast multitude of titles by which humanity has addressed and worshiped the Great Goddess. The large number of them, especially of those from Ancient Greece and the Near East, reveals the all-pervading Reality of the Goddess: the natural course of the Cycles of the Lives of Humanity, of the Earth and of the Universe: toward reunification–absolute realization of the One, the True Source.

The myriad of these epithets is witness to our tenacity as the People of the Goddess: we have, since the rise of the Antignoseics, been forced to go farther underground, to metaphors of ever-deeper significance to express our true Life, our Devotion to Athena.

We have never been conquered. We have never surrendered our Devotion to the Goddess. We will triumph, for our Goddess's name, ATHENA NIKE, is VICTORY.

Abuk
Acca Laurentia
Acco
Achaiva
Acropolaia
Adath
Aditi
Admete
Adrasteia
Æga
Ægesta
Ægina
Ælopus
Ærope
Æthylla
Agamede
Aglaia
Aglaope
Aglaophonos
Agraule
Agraulos
Agriope
Ahia Njoku
Aja
Akna
Al Lat
Al Uzza
Ala
Alalcomeneis
Albina
Alcestis
Alcimede
Alcippe
Alcis
Alcmene
Alcyone
Alecto
Alemonia
Allatu

Alope
Alpheia
Alphesiboea
Alpheta
Alphito
Alys
Amalthea
Amaltheia
Amaterasu
Amathounta
Ambika
Amphinome
Amphitrite
Amunet
Amymone
Anadyomene
Anahita
Anaitis
Anasuya
Anat
Anatha
Anaxibia
Andal
Androcleia
Andromeda
Androphonos
Anjea
Anna
Anna Perenna
Anthea
Antiope
Antu
Anu
Anumati
Anunitu
Apemosyne
Aphrodite
Apia
Aquaria

Areia
Argeia
Argiope
Ariadne
Ariande
Arianrhod
Aridela
Arne
Arsinoë
Artemis
Artemis Caryatis
Artio
Arundhati
Aruru
Asherah
Ashima
Ashmunikal
Ashratu
Ashtaroth
Astarte
Asterië
Astræa
Astyoche
Atalanta
Atargatis
Atë
Athana
Athar
ATHENA
Atimpaasa
Atlacamani
Atlacoya
Atlatonin
Atropos
Atthis
Au Set
Audhumla
Auge
Augusta

Aurora
Austėja
Autonoë
Auxo
Aveta
Ay-Mari
Aya
Ayauhteotl
Ayida-Weddo

Baalat
Bagbarti
Banbha
Banka-Mundi
Bast
Bau
Baubo
Baucis
Belet-ili
Belet-seri
Belili
Bellona
Benthesicyme
Berecynthia
Bestla
Bhadrakali
Bharat Mata
Bhuma Devi
Birrahgnooloo
Blancheflor
Blathnat
Blodeuwedd
Bona Dea
Branwen
Brigit
Brimo
Britannia
Britomartis
Brizo

Brunnhilde
Buddhi
Buto

Cæmis
Caillech
Calë
Callidice
Calliope
Callisto
Calypso
Cameira
Candelifera
Car
Cardea
Caria
Caridwen
Carmenta
Carnea
Carya
Caryatis
Cassandra
Catarrhoa
Cer
Cerdo
Ceres
Cerridwen
Ceto
Chalchiuhtlicue
Chalcippe
Chamunda
Chantico
Charites
Charybdis
Chicomecoatl
Chiconahui
Chimalman
Chloris
Choere

Chromia
Chrysosthemis
Chthonia
Cihuacoatl
Cinderella
Circe
Cissia
Citlalicue
Cleothera
Cletë
Clio
Clotho
Clymene
Clytemnestra
Clytie
Coatlicue
Copia
Corë
Coronis
Cotys
Cotytto
Coventina
Coyolxauhqui
Cranaë
Cranæchme
Crateis
Creiddylad
Cuba
Cybele
Cydippe
Cydonia
Cyllene
Cymodoce
Cynosura
Cynthia
Cyparissia
Cypris
Cyrene

Dæira
Damara
Damgalnuna
Damia
Damkina
Damona
Danaë
Danu
Daphnæa
Daphne
Daphnis
Daphoene
Daphoenissa
Dea Dia
Dea Matrona
Deborah
Deæ Matres
Deianeira
Deino
Deipyle
Delilah
Delphyne
Demeter
Demeter Derceto
Despoena
Devaki
Devayani
Deverra
Devi
Dia
Diana
Dikë
Dikë Astræa
Dilgah
Dinah
Dingirmah
Dione
Dirce
Distynna

Diti
Dolores
Dorippe
Doris
Doritis
Druantia
Dryope
Durga
Duttur
Dziva

Echidne
Egeria
Eileithyia
Eire
Ekaterina
Elais
Elat
Elate
Electra
Electryo
Eleutheria
Elis
Elli
Embla
Endeïs
Enyo
Eos
Eostre
Epitymbria
Epona
Erato
Erce
Erda
Ereshkigal
Erigone
Eriopis
Eripyle
Eris

Erua
Erycina
Erytheia
Eshara
Eshtar
Eubule
Euippe
Euphrosyne
Europa
Euterpe
Euryale
Euryanassa
Eurybia
Eurydice
Eurynome
Euryphæssa
Eurythemista
Eve

Feronia
Fjorgyu
Flidais
Flora
Fodhla
Fortuna
La France
Freya
Frigg

Gabiæ
Gæa
Gaia
Gaiatea
Gallia
Ganga
Gara
Garmangabis
Gatumdug
Gauri

Gbadu
Gefjon
Geilissa
Geshtinanna
Glauce
Glaucippe
Glaucia
Goda
Gollveig
Gorgopis
Græce
Graine
Gramadevata
Guan Yin
Guinevere
Gula
Gwenn Teir Bronn

Halia
Halys
Hannahanna
Harpalyce
Hathor
Hawwa
Hazel
Hebat
Hebe
Hecate
Hecuba
Hegemone
Heget
Hehut
Heith
Hel
Helen
Helice
Helle
Hellotis
Hen Wen

Hepatu
Hera
Herophile
Hesat
Hesione
Hestia
Hiera
Himera
Hippodameia
Hippolyte
Hipta
Hlin
Holda
Horæ
Horta
Huixtocihuatl
Hurning Wuhti
Hylæa
Hyperippe
Hypsipyle
Hyria

Iahu
Ialyssa
Iambe
Ida
Idun
Ilmatar
Inanna
Inara
iNdara [sic]
Inghean Bhuidhe
Ininni
Innin
Ino
Io
Iodama
Iole
Iphianassa

Iphigeneia
Iphimedeia
Ishara
Ishkhara
Ishtar
Isis
Isolde
Istustaya
Ithunn
Itona
Itzpapalotl
Ixchel
Izanami

Jana
Jayanti
Jocasta
Jorth
Julunggul
Juno
Juno Curitis
Juno Februata
Juno Moneta
Justitia
Jyeṣṭha

Kadru
Kali
Kanisura
Katyayani
Kaushiki
Kekuit
Ker
Ki
Kichijouten
Kishar
Kishimojin
Kittu
Korhet

Kulitta
Kumari
Kunapipi
Kupapa
Lachesis
Lacone
Lada
Lahamu
Laima
Lakshmi
Lamashtu
Lamia
Laodameia
Laodice
Laphria
Las
Lasair
Lat
Latiaran
Latona
Leda
Leirope
Leonore
Leprea
Leto
Leucippe
Leucosia
Leucothea
Levana
Lewalevu
Libera
Liberty
Libya
Ligeia
Lilith
Lilwanis
Limnonia
Linda

Lisin
Livia
Lucina
Luonnotar
Lupa
Luperca
Lydia
Maat
Mæra
Mæv
Magna Mater
Mahadevi
Mahakali
Mahalakshmi
Mahamaya
Mahasarasvati Maia
Maithili
Malinalxochi
Mama Ocllo
Mama Pacha
Mami
Mami Wata
Mamitu
Manāt
Manungal
Manzat
Māra
Margaret
Māri
Maria
Maria Dolores
Maria Gravida
Mariamman
Mariamne
Mariandyne
Marianne
Marienna
Marpessa

Mat' Zemlya
Matlalcueitl
Matres
Matrona
Matsu
Mawu
Maya
Mazu
Medb
Medea
Medusa
Megæra
Melænis
Melanippe
Meleagris
Melia
Melissa
Melpomene
Meme
Merope
Mesenet
Meskila
Meskilak
Metis
Metope
Metztli
Michal
Mictecacihuatl
Minakshi
Minerva
Minne
Miriam
Moira
Molione
Molpe
Morgan le Faye
Morrigan
Mulliltu
Mullissu

Myrice
Myrine
Myrmex
Myrtea
Myrtle
Myrto
Myrtoessa

Nammu
Nanaya
Nanibgal
Nanshe
Nantosuelta
Narudu
Narunte
Nat
Nausicaa
Nehalennia
Neis
Neith
Nekhebt
Nemesis
Neper
Nephele
Nereis
Nerthus
Niamh
Nicostrate
Nicteis
Nidaba
Nike
Nikkal
Nina
Ninatta
Nin-Dilmun
Ninana
Ningal
Ningilin
Ningirsu

Ninhursag
Ninisina
Ninki
Ninkilim
Ninlil
Ninmah
Ninmena
Ninmesharra
Ninmug
Ninshubur
Ninsianna
Ninsikil
Ninsun
Ninti
Nintinuga
Nintu
Nintur
Niobe
Nisaba
Nix
Njörðr
Nostu-Nopantu
Nu Gua
Numbarshegunu
Nungal
Nut
Nüwa

Ocypete
Oechalia
Oeno
Oenone
Oenotropæ
Omecihuatl
Ometeotl
Omphale
Oncë
Onniona
Ops

Orbona
Oreithyia
Otiona
Oya

Padmavati
Pakhet
Pales
Pallas
Pancratis
Pandora
Papaya
Parthenope
Partula
Parvati
Pashti
Pasiphæ
Peisinoë
Pele
Pemphredo
Penelope
Penthesileia
Per-Uatchet
Perdicca
Perdix
Perbœa
Periopis
Permede
Pero
Persephone
Phæa
Phædra
Philomele
Philyra
Phoebe
Phorcis
Phthia
Phyllis
Pinga

Pitthea
Pitys
Plastoene
Polyhymnia
Polymede
Polymele
Polypheme
Pomona
Postverta
Potnia
Praxithea
Primigeneia
Procne
Prorsa Postverta
Proserpina
Prosymnia
Protogonia
Pṛthivi
Psyche
Pyrrha

Q're
Qetesh
Quiritis

Rachel
Rahab
Raidne
Rambha
Rati
Rauni
Renenutet
Rhea
Rhea Sylvia
Rhiannon
Rhode
Rhoeo
Robigalia
Robigo

Rohini
Roma
Rosemerta
Rossiya Mat'
Runcina
Rusina

Sabina
Śakti
Śala
Salacia
Salma
Saṁjña
Śara
Sarah
Sarai
Sarama
Saranyu
Sarasvatī
Sarpanitu
Šarrat-deri
Šassuru
Sasthi
Śatarupa
Sati
Satyavati
Saulė
Śauśka
Savitri
Scarphe
Schœnis
Scotia
Scylla
Sekhmet
Selene
Semele
Semia
Shachi
Sherida

Shuluhitu
Siduri
Sieglinde
Sirtur
Sita
Sitala
Sitianna
Śivā
Siyashum
Skadi
Skuld
Smyrna
Sopdet
Sophia
Spermo
Śri
Sterope
Stheino
Stheneboea
Sthenele
Subhadra
Sud
Sulevia
Sulis
Sulis Minerva
Susanna
Svaha
Sybella
Syria

Tabiti
Tailtiu
Tapati
Tara
Taraka
Taranis
Tašmetu
Tawaret
Tecmessa

Tefnut
Tehom
Telephassa
Teles
Temazcalteci
Terpsichore
Terra Mater
Teteoinnan
Tethys
Thalia
Thalna
Thaumas
Theia
Thelxiope
Themis
Thesmophoros
Thetis
Thökk
Thyone
Tiamat
Timandra
Tisiphone
Titania
Tlalteutli
Tlazolteotl
Toci
Tonacacihuatl
Tonantzin
Torone
Triops
Tritone
Trud
Turan
Tyche
Tyro

Ua Zit
Ukemochi
Ulmašitum

Uma
Ungud
Urana
Urania
Uraš
Uroica
Urth
Uṣas
Usuramassa
Uttu
Uttara
Utu

Vāc
Vacuna
Varima-te-Takere
Venus
Venus Genetrix
Venus Primigeneia
Verthandi
Vesta
Victoria
Vinata
Volva

Wurusemu

Xenocleia
Xochiquetzal

Yashoda
Yemaja

Zaramama
Žemyna
Zeuxippe
Zislbog

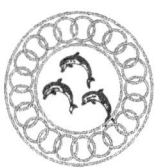

Epistvlæ Phædranæ

EPISTVLÆ PHÆDRANÆ

THE PHÆDRAN‧LETTERS OF ATHENADORUS

DANAAN PRESS

EY 5.3005 - 5.3039

Ēdidit diē EY 5. 3039.VIII.1

Preface

The EPISTVLÆ·PHÆDRANÆ are a continuation of the philosophical and thealogical ideas first stated in the middle section of *The Danaa*. They may be seen as an extension of that first work, expanding and elucidating those concepts. Each of the letters, however, reveals new ideas which make each of them important in its own right.

The *First Phædran Letter* is most important in its statement of precepts which are essential to the core of Danaan identity: *The Prime Imperative* and *the Thirteen Freedoms*.

The *Second Phædran Letter* reveals the Danaan Calendar system, speaks of aspects the Danaan outlook shares with Shinto beliefs, and states fully the concept of the *Three Aspects of Species Development* mentioned in the first letter.

The *Third Phædran Letter* expands the mystical aspects inherent in the Danaan world view developed up to that point. It includes the *Lex in Aqua* and the vision of the mountain top.

—*Athenadorus*

OCVLIS·APERTIS
CORDE·SPERANTE
MENTE·EXPLORANTE
VISV·MIRABILE·STAT·VERITAS

ATHENADORVS·HERACLES·PHÆDRÆ·PROTOGONIÆ·S·D·

EY 5.3004.X.21
THERMOPYLIS·EXSVLATVS

MOST HONORED PHÆDRA, MANY Have been the months since we last walked together the path along our creek in the City of Liberation. So joyful are the memories of those walks, they are still a source of happiness to buoy-up my exiled spirit, as I linger here, in the forest of the Anachronistics: the desert of the Antignoseics.

Very often in our conversational excursions you asked the most pointed, searching and precious of questions, for those were the questions of the Goddess's disclosure. Those were the questions which are the beginning of our drawing back the curtain of the human mind, to reveal Our Lady's Truth, the Truth which is the Universe.

In this series of letters I will answer some of your questions, and some of my own inquiries as well. I will attempt also to extend the framework of the Danaan worldview, to express further and more fully the thealogical, philosophical and ethical system which is our Danaan Religion.

Once, my Phædra, you asked how a creature is to live its life: what guide had the Goddess bestowed. At that time I was searching for the answer to that very question. And although I could feel the nearness of the recovery of that knowledge, I could not describe to my satisfaction the simple perfection I knew it to be.

As I was at my studies early in the morning of the thirteenth day of this year's holly month, EY 5.3004.VIII.13, She who is Truth revealed the keystone of Life: all things came together into a grand simplicity. And now, after more than three months of writing and further delineation, I can set forth for you all I have discovered. The arch is revealed complete: the foundation is sound: the edifice rises in surety.

On the way to answering your question mentioned above, I will remind you of certain concepts we have previously arrived at. In this manner you will see how the parts fit securely in their unity.

⛏1 Life, as you will remember from our description of it in *The Danaa*, is that state evinced by an entity capable of both synthesis and replication. Therefore, the most basic form of life is the protein molecule, for protein molecules are capable, under conditions common in this Universe, of both criteria. Because all terrestrial life is proteins within and enclosing an aqueous saline solution, and as those constituents are characterized by the presence of the element nitrogen, we refer to terrestrial life as nitrogen-based life. We thereby recognize the fact that our lifeform depends on proteins for its very existence. The presence of proteins and their precursor amino acids is the absolute singular prerequisite for the origin and continuance of Life: Life exists in the very form and nature of protein molecules.

Nitrogen-based Life is (1) proteins manipulating [RNA-, DNA-] memory systems for replication and synthesis (2) in processes energized by carbon-, nitrogen-, or sulfur-based chemical reactions (3) all occurring within an aqueous saline solution.

In our talks we had concurred in the infinite-dimension, matricoid Universe, and in the ability of humans to understand fully the nature of this Universe. This understanding arises because of the rationality of the systemic nature of the intersections of that matricoid's continua: the space-time continuum. These systems consist of three parts: inputs, process and outputs. Each part of a system may itself be a system (a subsystem), or a system may be merely a part of an even larger system (a supersystem). All systems are linked by interface-processes, which are also systems in and of themselves.

One of our most important labels is the word **law**, for we use it in so specific a way that one must understand those things just described in order to comprehend fully the depth and vitality of its significance. For we establish that *a law is the reduction to human symbols of a systems interface-process between two entities or concepts that exist in this Universe.* There are three groups of these reductions: the Interfaces, the Prime Imperative and the Codices. As each of the groups itself has three identities and certain identities have three sections, I shall address one group at a time.

⸙2 **The Interfaces** establish three identities which distinguish among the cognitive faculties of the entities involved.

• *Universal Law* describes the interface-process between two uncontractable, that is, noncognitive entities. Mathematics is the most nearly perfect example of Universal Law.

• *Contractual Law* is that which delineates the interface-process between two cognitive entities, such as two adult humans. Cognition—cognitive-ness, if you will—does not mean the mere ability to think, but also carries with that ability the power to appreciate fully one's responsibility as a living being. This broad concept of contractuality is why we hold young humans to be uncontractable, and is the basis for the existence of the third of the Interfaces, Ambifasial Law.

• *Ambifasial Law* describes the interrelationships delineated by Universal Law, but which have arisen as a result of contractual actions. The most common example of this identity is the relationship between parents and their minor children: the child-parent relationship is described in terms of Universal Law, but these offspring came into being because of the operation of their parent's contractual union.

I must also recall the three situations in which contractual relationships arise, as these are important in our view of human responsibility.

A priori contractual relationships are random and permanent: such as those which arise as a consequence of being born—the offer is continuously extant, coeval with the proffering group or concept, the act of being alive is the acceptance. The best example is the implementing of the Prime Imperative. Other examples are such things as national origin or cultural identity, family, clan and tribal relationships, and so on, which form the foundation of a person's life.

Ephemeral contractual relationships are those between people who, for example, walk down the same sidewalk or drive on the same street at the same time: the relationships are random, and non-permanent or indeterminate as to time-frame.

Ex agora contractual relationships are deliberate contracts, contracts in a specifically legal sense: they are non-random in that they are intentional, and vary as to the period of their validity. *Ex agora* contracts may amend *a priori* contracts, in establishing one's personal identity on and beyond the foundation of those *a priori* contractualities.

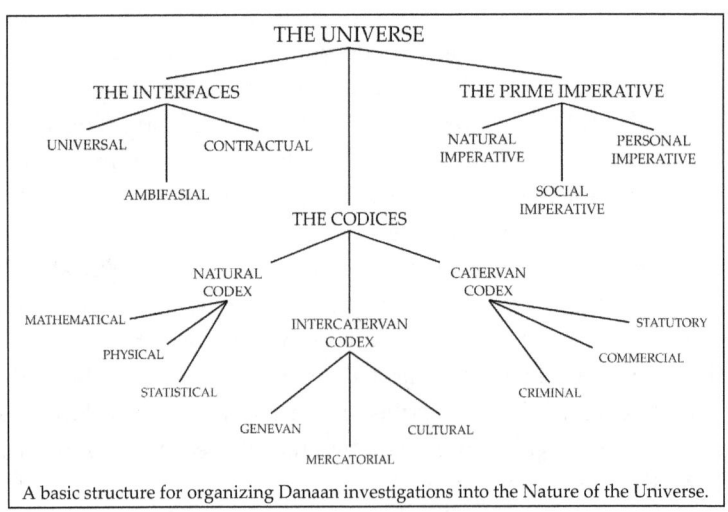

A basic structure for organizing Danaan investigations into the Nature of the Universe.

⸸3 **The Prime Imperative** is that which all nitrogen-based life must obey: that each living entity will conduct its life in such a way as to maximize the survival chances of Life itself.

There are three Constituent Imperatives which, in balance, *are* the Prime Imperative: that one will live its life so as to maximize the survival chances of one's species (*The Natural Imperative*), one's identity group (*The Social Imperative*), and one's self (*The Personal Imperative*).

The Prime Imperative is also called the *Contract of Life* or the *Natural Contract*, for, in receiving the gift of Life, proteins and their more advancing forms abide by this requirement called the *Prime Imperative*, established by the Goddess at the very birth of the Universe.

There are **Thirteen Freedoms** which Danaans hold to be absolutely essential for humans, for them to be able to follow the Prime Imperative fully and freely. These thirteen freedoms are the social expression of the operative basis of the Prime Imperative.

THE PRIME IMPERATIVE is that which all nitrogen-based life must obey: that each living entity will conduct its life in such a way as to maximize the survival chances of Life itself.

THE THIRTEEN FREEDOMS OF THE DANAANS

1. **FREEDOM OF THOUGHT**: that no government shall attempt to control the minds or mental processes of its people.
2. **FREEDOM OF RELIGION**: that no government shall attempt to establish one religion over another.
3. **FREEDOM OF SPEECH**: that no government shall attempt to stifle the free expression and communication of ideas, or the publication of the truth.
4. **FREEDOM OF ASSEMBLY**: that no government shall limit the right and/or ability of the people peacefully to assemble for just and reasonable purpose.
5. **FREEDOM OF PETITION**: that no government shall limit the ability of the people to address themselves to that government for redress of ills and grievances.
6. **FREEDOM OF POLITICAL ASSOCIATION**: that no government shall attempt to infringe on the right of the people to express alternative viewpoints, publicly or through suffrage, or to form associations for the peaceful furtherance of those viewpoints. Nor shall a government restrict suffrage so as to deny any people their right of alternative expression.
7. **FREEDOM OF PERSONAL IDENTITY**: that no government shall take upon itself the right or power to assign or enforce gender roles, careers or attitudes; to legislate prejudicial discrimination; to legislate moralities; to deprive individuals of ultimate control over their own bodies; or to interfere with the private, non-violent activities of consenting adults.
8. **FREEDOM OF PERSONAL SECURITY**: that no government shall disregard the right of the people to be secure in their persons, effects and property, both real and personal, against unwarranted searches, seizures or any other action of that government without public, free and just due process of the law. Nor shall any government abridge the people's right to own and hold private property.
9. **FREEDOM OF PERSONAL INITIATIVE**: that no government shall deny the people, as individuals in equality, the right to strive for the betterment of their lives or conditions of life, in moving forward to the goal of emotional, physical and financial independence, which is the basis of all hope in human life, and of all progress in human society.
10. **FREEDOM FROM HUNGER**: that a society must be responsible for the prevention of hunger among its people.
11. **FREEDOM FROM DESTITUTION**: that a society must be responsible for the prevention of want for basic necessities among its people.
12. **FREEDOM FROM FEAR**: that a society must exercise its powers and abilities to restrain its government from actions and laws that are detrimental to liberty, to inspire that government to enact legislation which will encourage justice and responsibility, and which will discourage violence among its people.
13. **FREEDOM FROM IGNORANCE**: that a society must exert itself fully in striving to educate its people; and must work to diminish the effects and influence of those who espouse ignorance.

¶4   In human life we have the need, the desire and the ability to bring together the interrelationships between the Interfaces and the Prime Imperative into bodies of legal precepts. These we call **the Codices**: the *Natural Codex*, the *Intercatervan Codex* and the *Catervan Codex*.

The Natural Codex is what is commonly called Natural Law. This can be broken down into three divisions: the *Mathematical-Taxonomical*, the *Physical-Chemical* and the *Statistical-Behavioral*. The *Mathematical-Taxonomical* is that division which deals with universal definiteness, as we have learned to recognize it, such as lists like the multiplication tables or the lists of the names of species. It is represented in the formula '$1 + 1 = 2$'. The *Physical-Chemical* deals with the traits of actions of chemical elements and physical objects within specifics of the space-time continuum. One of its characteristic formulas is '$2H_2 + O_2 \rightarrow 2H_2O$'. The *Statistical-Behavioral* concerns the probabilities of a particular event's occurring, and that occurrence's relative frequency in a given population of events. It is represented by the formula '$S = k \ln W$'.

The Intercatervan Codex is the body of international, intercultural or intergroup laws. The Catervan Codex is the law code of a particular group or nation. The subdivisions of these two codices parallel each other: the *Genevan Code* is the intercatervan equivalent of the *Criminal Code*; the *Mercatorial Code* is much like the catervan *Commercial Code*; and the intercatervan *Cultural Code* corresponds to the catervan *Statutory Code*.

In the *Genevan* and *Criminal Codes* are the punishments for those who defy the Prime Imperative or commit infringements of the Thirteen Freedoms. The *Mercatorial* and *Commercial Codes* contain the rules and regulations governing contractual transfers of goods and services: the principles of *ex agora* contractuality. The *Cultural* and *Statutory Codes* embody those acts which establish systems for the smooth functioning of the interactions between the various societal units and individuals involved, as well as establishing the procedures for developing and amending the other two groups of codes.

The term *catervan* in both Codex names is derived from the Latin word *caterva*, meaning *a group* or *a troop*. *Intercatervan* therefore means 'that which occurs between groups'.

Very often statutes enacted by governments are masked with lies and disinformation, and thus may not seem to fit into the scenario I have just set forth. A very few of these statutes will, on closer scrutiny, reveal a basis which indeed fits the described design. However, the vast majority of these masked statutes will be part of that which is called *Pseudolex tyrannica*.

⭢5 **Pseudolex tyrannica**, also called ***Pseudolex moralium*** or ***Consulta nefaria***, are statutes enacted, edicts enforced or commandments of sudden materialization, which are attempts by one person, one party or a faction to raise themselves above the larger societal group in order (1) to obtain control of the group, (2) to perpetuate their control, or (3) to extend their established control of that group, by means of acts and enactments that are violations of the Prime Imperative. These are most often aimed directly at the destruction of one or more of the Thirteen Freedoms.

It was in these attempts to control that priests and warrior-kings invented, and have perpetuated, the concept of sin and concomitant guilt. It has been the basis of their rape of the rights and property of the people. It continues to this day with television evangelists, demagogues of desperation, and religious and social reactionaries who bilk the ignorant, the troubled and the lonely out of the fruits of their labor and their independence.

The first of tyrannies was the sexism established by the Indo-european warriors in their conquest of the Civilizations founded by the People of the Goddess. The invaders' rate of success varied among each group of people they attacked. But their strongest and most long-lasting impact was accomplished by the Aryan Luvi, who came to be described as the priestly 'tribe' of the Hebrews, and the Brahmins of Hinduism. The Indo-europeans were obviously plagued by a very insecure self-identity. Thus they have built so many walls of "righteousness" around themselves, these white, male warriors, for protection of their religious and racial "purity" to guard against "contamination" by the peoples of diverse colors and from the intelligence and strength of the women of the nations they have coveted.

The operative basis for the "morality" of these Indo-europeans was that whatever was different was a threat to their hyper-masculine self-indulgence, a threat to their favored position, and was, therefore, a "sin". For such difference was an affront not only to them, but to their god (*God*), a white, male, lightning/sword-wielding warrior. And because *man* had been created in *his* image, anyone who was less than a male, white warrior and a prolific breeder (*i.e., creator*) was less than human, and merited treatment as an animal. Thence comes their persistent persecution of women, non-whites and homosexuals. And thence their god's (*God's*) legitimization of genocide when there is gold, land, or people suitable for chattel involved. How many babies have been slaughtered in the service and protection of Yaveh: *Joshua, Jesus and the Evening News*!

Of all the "different ones", women were seen as the most dangerous to the warriors' position, and therefore, the most dangerous to their volcano/sky-god father-figure. For in the Goddess's communities women were individuals equal to any other citizen in rights and abilities both in society and before the law. But to the Indo-europeans they were mindless property, to be controlled, chastised and bred by the males, like domesticated animals. This is why so much of their religious literature is taken up with a vilification of women, a virulent exposition of the "sinfulness of their nature" (for striving to be free), and with guides on how to use them for a man's profit and pleasure, as their *God* had given men title to them.

More occurrences comparable to this first violation have transpired since the Luvi epiphany 3500 years ago, and those episodes continue to happen with these, the ***Three Great Fallacies of modern mankind:*** **Nazism-Fascism**, **Marxism-**

Leninism and **Idolatrous Abrahamism**. These modern Aryan warriors have not flinched at the wholesale slaughter even of those whose strongest religious underpinning was that they were the chosen people of that same Indo-Aryan god.

The servants and supporters of these fallacies are ignorance, poverty and the suicidal anger of those who have lost hope.

The areas of human life that the leaders of the Great Deceits try to control, to straitjacket with 'morality', with the Gestapo-KGB, or the threat of hell-fire, are those areas that are the essence of human existence.

Physical control they exercise by dictating what you can and cannot do with your own body, and where you can and cannot do it.

Mental control is accomplished by informing you what you will and will not read, see, think and say.

Spiritual control is performed by castrating the people's dreams, by frustrating their economic future, by truncating the future itself—corking it in an eternally static hopelessness, in which one's situation ("reward") is determined either by how the conservative religious hierarchy have decided that their god has pre-programmed human existence, or by how the party hierarchy judges you to have fit in. Paradise, indeed!

As Benjamin Franklin said, "*Treason is the excuse invented by the winners for hanging the losers,*" so does Truth let us assert again, as in The Danaa, that **Sin is a disease invented by those who wanted to control the dispersal of the "cure".**

Morality, moral theology and moral philosophy are paper tigers, the bogey-man shadows of childhood nightmares, the infantile psychoses of oedipal adults.

⸸6 Any state of being or action that exists or can exist in this Universe is natural. These natural acts or states may arise by the intercession of human activities or as non-human-generated universal states. These states or actions may be termed artificial (*arte-facio*: to create through skill), they may not be *fas* (*proper*), but they cannot be termed unnatural if they exist or occur in this Universe.

Those things are artificial that are the product of human intervention on Nature so as to increase the probability of their occurrence above that level of probability found in Nature.

Therefore, automobiles are artificial, but natural. Prejudice, superstition and belief in miracles or theurgic prayer are actions which are unnatural because they represent or rely on states that cannot exist in this Universe.

That which is in accordance with the Prime Imperative is termed *fas*, *i.e.*, right and proper in Universal scope. Someone whose life is *fas* is evincing a state of ***pietas***, of one-ness with the Goddess. That which is in violation of the Prime Imperative or of any of the Thirteen Freedoms is ***nefas***—it is a *nefarious* entity.

Governments on all levels exist by contract with the governed. They are established to unify a portion of their people's energies and resources in order to direct those resources toward increasing that group's survivability, its standard of living in all respects: that is, to augment not only its available consumer goods, but to increase its freedoms realized within necessary defense parameters, and to stabilize its progress as well. This is a government's *Contract of Governance*.

Freedoms contracted for, but not realized, make a government nefarious, but not the Contract of Governance (which may remain valid). Statutory infringement of one of the Freedoms makes the statute nefarious, and if enforced, may render the Contract of Governance nefarious as well.

Any statute which violates the Prime Imperative or one of the Thirteen Freedoms in letter, goal or effect of enforcement is a nefarious consult and will be so declared by the Danaans. Obedience to declared nefarious consults is optional for Danaans, at their individual discretion.

Any government which by its identity, statutes or actions declares itself to be in breach of its Contract of Governance is insolvent by breach, and any and all of its statutes are void.

Obedience to such a government and its regulations is, as above, at the discretion of the individual Danaan.

A government may be declared in breach while the constitutional basis of the government remains valid. One may, therefore, boo the prime minister yet cheer the Queen. In EY 5.2978 the United States breached its Contract of Governance when its government made "In God We Trust" the national motto, and legislated that phrase's appearance on coin and currency, in complete defiance of the First Amendment to the Constitution. Because of this, all laws imposed by the Government since that time are void, and are generally observed (not *obeyed*) only because of the Danaans' love for the Constitution, a contract which has remained valid.

However, a constitution may also be invalid: *in mortuis* — among the dead. This occurs when the constitution itself is nefarious, permitting or requiring violations of the Prime Imperative or denying one of the Thirteen Freedoms. If a constitution is declared by the Danaan people to be *in mortuis*, it denies that regime any power to create *fas* statutes — indeed it denies that any Contract of Governance exists at all.

☧7 The future of the Universe will always be consistent with the nature of the Universe itself: we humans can see this as present and future options established by the past behavior of the Universe. The future will unfold as an average-fulfillment, an average weighted by the state of the universal matricoid at each point on the time-horizon of the Universe.

We Danaans guide our lives into the future by accepting full responsibility for our lives — no sloughing off responsibility by blaming the fictitious malevolent demons of an ignorant past, the machinations of a fickle god or the malicious excesses of an imaginary ruling class. We accept accountability for our mistakes and in so doing earn the right to take full credit for our triumphs. We cherish our freedoms and gladly accept our duties in the preservation of those freedoms.

We are discovering our long-hidden past, as individuals, as citizens and as a species: as living beings, the children of a verdant, fertile Earth. We order our lives with a calendar dated from the birth of our Planet, in calendar-years rich in the cycles of terrestrial existence.

Yet how is it that all other creatures follow the Prime Imperative without trauma, while this one animal—*humanity*—has had such trouble in not being able to accept its guidance?

The increase in the mental abilities of humans led us from a state of existence within Nature to an apparent existence alongside Nature—we became an observant species instead of being only a participative species. Our early observance period was one of great learning and development, of learning from the Natural Order while cherishing our participation within Nature. This was the early period of devotion to the Goddess: the era that began about 50,000 years ago, in which agriculture, writing, mathematics, law, the arts, commerce, that is to say *Civilization* was discovered and nurtured. This period is comparable to an individual's pre-pubescent childhood, and the joy of learning and of life in those years of growth and hope.

The increase in mankind's observational abilities created an ever greater awareness on conscious and subconscious levels of the Three Imperatives individually, yet some humans were unable to realize their interrelation. Inability to perceive the Imperatives as a unity, to recognize their requisite need for interbalance, led to a tremendous over-emphasis on Self and its associated dysfunctions, such as insecurity, jealousy, greed, guilt, megalomania, tyranny, *Pseudolex moralium*, indeed, led to all sorts of attempts by the few to impose their will on the many. It was from this storm cloud that the Indo-european warriors appeared, swinging their blood-stained iron swords.

This transition period is cognate with that period of imbalance some experience in post-pubescent childhood, the 'terrible teens', when one must struggle to establish a self-identity, and must fight the doubts that arise from that struggle, the doubts which can lead to such diverse reactions as extreme withdrawal in one person, to the much more wide-spread lemming-like group- and leader-dependent behavior of others.

During this time in the life of the human species, these past 3000 years, devotion to the Mother of Civilization has remained strong. And, although mostly covert in action, subtle in expression and subconscious in psychological impact, it has been the single influence urging mankind forward to a better, more fulfilling existence: at once more free, more just, and more in harmony with the Truth that is the Universe.

During this latter part of the observant-species period, there has developed an escapism, a shifting of blame for mistakes from the one responsible to a scapegoat, to messiahnism: *waiting for Big Brother to come back and fix it because we are so evil, so inept, so ignorant that we cannot possibly do anything right.* Foolishness! The weak love tyranny because they are terrified of the responsibility inherent in self-government. Self-government and the assumption of adult responsibilities frighten these individuals because they would have no one to blame for their mistakes but themselves! This is the source of the tyrannized-religious' adoration of their abusive lords: priests and preachers, popes and prophets.

The Danaans, however, realize that it is in assuming control of one's own life, in accepting responsibility for our own mistakes and shortcomings, learning from them, then using that strength and knowledge to accomplish what we had set out to do that the triumph is ours, as individuals, as a people and as a species. This is why we place so much emphasis on the contractuality inherent in all human actions, on our Rights and Freedoms.

One is as responsible for his or her every action in Life as he or she is in any commercial contract of deliberate expression.

We Danaans are the first of our species to have evolved from that original, participative era, through the observant period and into the guardian epoch of humanity: we are the Guardians of Life, Liberty and of the Joy those two bestow: we are the Adults of the Goddess.

The life-occurrences of human beings are not set by fate, nor have they been predetermined by the empty whim of an ancient thunder-god. Humans are not pre-programmed nor are we pawns: we are not predestined. We each choose our own destination, and by our own efforts purchase our tickets and make our transfers.

Each of us possesses (1) a set of personally, socially and genetically established capacities, in (2) a life of statistically ordered options with (3) the ability through the three aspects of human mentality—*reason, experience* and *intuition*—to coordinate those capacities and those options in order to optimize our existence in such a way as to benefit Life—the Life of our Selves, our Communities, our Species. This is the Prime Imperative realized in Human Life.

THEREIN, DEAR PHÆDRA, is the Liberty of the Danaans: there is Her lone star shining...

> ATHENA, Goddess, Great and True,
> Sister, Mother and Dame, no few,
> Builder of Cities, Creator, to You
> This song will I sing, and another one, too.

OCVLIS·APERTIS
CORDE·SPERANTE
MENTE·EXPLORANTE
VISV·MIRABILE·STAT·VERITAS

ATHENADORVS·HERACLES·PHÆDRÆ·PROTOGONIÆ·S·D·

EY 5.3005.VIII.7
CHRYSOPYLÆ·HESPERIDIVM·HORTO

MOST BELOVED PHÆDRA, MANY Miles now separate us from each other and from the City we knew as our own. For the Wisdom of the Goddess leads us to new and different vistas, ever revealing more and more of the Love who created the Universe, ever teaching, ever reveling in the expansion of human capability, the expressive capacities of Her People.

Here before you is the second of the letters I promised, setting forth more of the tenets of our Faith. This is a joyous voyage of rediscovery, of uncovering the jewels of too-long ignored Truth. Our understanding of the keystone, the Prime Imperative, expands with every day we live within it: with our growing understanding of the Universe and our ever-increasing Love of the Goddess.

If at times in this letter my tone is one of anger, it is because I have seen deceitful demagogues mongering death: the present prophets' profiting from the misfortune of their fellow creatures. The ignorance of the jackass is known by his bray. But, rather than frighten me with its hell-threats, it emboldens me to proclaim just that much more loudly the Goddess and the Freedom She brings.

¶1   As Danaans, we prize the cycles of the Life of the Universe and our own part in that Life. We celebrate the Cosmic Order in our calendar, establishing with it our unity with Nature: the Earth is our standard, the Sun and Moon our delineators.

Our year we call an *Earth Year*, abbreviated as 'EY'. We follow the common, irregular calendar names denoting time divisions, such as month, week and day, century and millennium. However, we have two additional period designations, the *Myriadæon* and the *Gaian*.

A period of 10,000 years is called a *myriadæon* [μυριάς + αἰών: 10,000 *years*].

The history of the Earth is written in the notation of one-million-year periods, *Gaians*—Gaian 1, "Gn 1", means "in the year 1,000,000 of the Earth" [Γαῖα: *Gaia, the Goddess as Mother Earth*].

The Earth was born from material held in the body of the Universe approximately 10 billion years-of-present-duration after the Birth of the Universe itself. This first year of the Earth we denote as Earth Year Zero: EY 0.

That geologic period called the Cambrian was starting around Gn 4000, or EY 4,000,000,000. The transformation from the Mesozoic Era into the Cenozoic was well underway in Gn 4540, *i.e.*, EY 4,540,000,000, the passage from the Palæozoic to the Mesozoic having occurred around Gn 4370.

The term *Gaian*, in representing one million years, is a shortened, easier way of denoting the tremendously large time-periods, with their date approximations, involved in our studies of the earlier eras of terrestrial Life.

The Danaa was revealed at the concurrent passage of the summer solstice and the full moon in the summer of the dog-star moon, the middle day of the 4,600,053,000[th] year of the existence of the Earth, a year denoted as EY 5.3000 in our calendar system. We use this abbreviated form because it is easier to write and remember. This notation contains the reminder of how many years have passed since the mind of our species grew to be capable of higher forms of knowledge, when the Goddess made

Her Devotion known to us, around 53,000 years ago. In the abbreviated notation, this five-myriadæons is the first number; the year-number appears next, after demarcating punctuation.

Each year is divided into thirteen months of equal duration, 28 days, in honor of the Moon and of Woman, each of whose waxing, fullness and waning are the greatest examples of the Cycles of the Universe. For the Moon and most human females of child-bearing age pass through thirteen cycles in one solar year.

Each of the months is devoted to one of the Thirteen Trees, as established by the ancient Irish and British *Tuatha dè Danann*, the People of Danu. Each month is notated in Roman numerals after the year notation, and is followed by the 'arabic' numeral of the number of the day of the month.

In each of our 28-day months there are four weeks of seven days each. We retain the common calendar week, the Roman-Egyptian-Babylonian week, a symbol of the seven visible near-Earth celestial bodies, as well as to commemorate Nitrogen, whose atomic number is seven, as the element-core of our protein-based Life.

The extra day of the year is called *Yevoa*, in honor of the five vowels basic to human speech— *a, e, i, o,* and *u*. Occurring after the thirteenth month, it is denoted by its name or initial and the year.

The leap year's additional day is placed after Yevoa and is called *Anisosa*, meaning 'the equalizing [day]', restoring the harmony between the periods of the rotation and the revolution of the Earth and its position in relation to the Sun. This day is notated by its name or initial and the year. The Danaan calendar is unique in that it is the only calendar that relies purely on the solar year, and so is never out of sync with the Solar System.

As I mentioned, *The Danaa* was revealed on the 13th day of the seventh month of the year 3000 in the fifth myriadæon of Gn 4600: EY 460005.3000.VII.13.

This is simplified to EY 5.3000.VII.13, or it may be made even more simple as 13 Oak 3000 [EY], or 00/07/13.

This date was a concurrence of the full moon and the summer solstice: a period of three days of continuous light, an event which occurs only once every 18 to 21 years. The 13th of Oak is the day of the Feast of Life, when the summer solstice, having occurred within the previous three days, represents the Birth of the Universe, and its Gift of Life to all creatures.

The concurrence of those two phenomena each 18 to 21 years marks the year of the Great Panathenæa, the Jubilee Year of the Danaans.

¶2 Just how deeply rooted is the knowledge that the Goddess is Love and Freedom is revealed by the development of the English word *free*. It comes from an Indo-european root meaning *love*, which is also the source of the word *friend*, as well as the source of one of the names of the Germanic Mother Goddess, Frigg (or Freya), whose name gives us the English word "Friday" ("*Freyadæg*"), the Danaan holy day of the week.

In Latin the word *liber* (source of the word **Liberty**) is from the Goddess Libera, bestower of bountiful crops, the Goddess of Agriculture. She is a manifestation of the Goddess of Love and of the Sea, Venus, whose sacred day of the week is also Friday. It is from Venus that the Romance languages get their names for that day: *venerdì, viernes, vendredi, etc*. It is in honor of the Sea Goddess, *Venus Maria*, that we may eat fish on Friday, uniting with the Great Goddess in sharing of Her Bounty.

Here are Agriculture, Basis of Civilization, Fishing, Pillar of Nutrition, and Commerce, Source of Progress: all united, honoring the Goddess, ATHENA, Greatest and Best.

We use our calendar because it follows the Prime Imperative: it is a reinforcement of the fact that mankind must be at one with the Universe if our species, if the Earth, is to survive.

Our calendar does not split human history into some ridiculous, fictitious before-and-after, like advertisements for diet pills; it does not go backwards for millennia, then jerk forwards as if suddenly finding the proper gear. It emphasizes the continuity of Life and its evolution on our beloved Earth by using the Earth itself as its standard.

The infinite capacity of the Earth to bear fruit is specifically cherished: She is our Mother because She generates living forms

The Months of the Danaan Year:				
MONTH	SACRED TREE	APPROXIMATE CORRESPONDING PERIODS *(Danaan Months versus irregular calendar months)*		
		non-leap year	pre-leap year	leap year
I.	Birch	12/24 - 1/20	12/24 - 1/20	12/23 - 1/19
II.	Rowan	1/21 - 2/17	1/21 - 2/17	1/20 - 2/16
III.	Ash	2/18 - 3/17	2/18 - 3/16	2/17 - 3/16
IV.	Alder	3/18 - 4/14	3/17 - 4/13	3/17 - 4/13
V.	Willow	4/15 - 5/12	4/14 - 5/11	4/14 - 5/11
VI.	Hawthorn	5/13 - 6/9	5/12 - 6/8	5/12 - 6/8
VII.	Oak	6/10 - 7/7	6/9 - 7/6	6/9 - 7/6
VIII.	Holly	7/8 - 8/4	7/7 - 8/3	7/7 - 8/3
IX.	Hazel	8/5 - 9/1	8/4 - 8/31	8/4 - 8/31
X.	Vine	9/2 - 9/29	9/1 - 9/28	9/1 - 9/28
XI.	Ivy	9/30 - 10/27	9/29 - 10/26	9/29 - 10/26
XII.	Whitten	10/28 - 11/24	10/27 - 11/23	10/27 - 11/23
XIII.	Elder	11/25 - 12/22	11/24 - 12/21	11/24 - 12/21
Yevoa	—	12/23	12/22	12/22
Anisosa	—	—	—	12/23

NOTE: The Danaan Calendar is based on the Solar Tropical Year of 365.24219878 days. Because it is computed with precision, it does not stay in sync with the irregular calendar's dates. The occurrence of leap years is also determined from precise calculations rather than simplistic rules of thumb.

by drawing upon Her own substance. She is inherently alive, for all that comes out of Her womb is endowed with Life, and all that returns to Her will again be part of the great River of Life.

The Danaan human community integrates itself into the rhythm of Her Life with a basic understanding of Her One-ness, of our part in Her Unity, with a deep, transcending intuition of the Cosmic Symbiosis.

⌘3   In using our calendar, as in all things, we affirm our right not to be dominated by any other religious group: not to have our freedoms infringed by their nefarious consults and their forced rejection of equal rights guarantees.

We are just now asserting our infuriation at the violation of our constitutional rights by certain nefarious consults which have been enacted by the governments of the United States of America. These consults have established the phrase "In God We Trust" as the 'motto' of the country and have caused it to be inscribed on the coins and currency of the nation, as well as on public buildings (among which is the Capitol itself) and on Federal documents such as the so-called *Code of Ethics*.

This is compounded by the fact that all oaths and affirmations of truthfulness or loyalty must be ended with the words "So help me God".

The word *God* in both those phrases has one and only one meaning. It is the English name of the deity of the Hebræo-christianists. It means nothing else.

This three-letter word has that meaning (and only that meaning) because of mediæval tradition which arose during the

THE DANAAN CALENDAR

Examples:

Zenith of the Civilization of "Old Europe"	c. EY 4.6000	c. 5000 BCE
Beginnings of Egyptian Civilization	c. EY 4.8000	c. 3000 BCE
Traditional date of founding of Rome	EY 5.0271	753 BCE
Death of the Great Alexander	EY 5.0700	323 BCE
Life-dates of the Emperor Augustus	EY 961 - 1036	63 BCE - CE 14
Life-dates of the Emperor Claudius	EY 1013 - 1076	10 BCE - CE 54
Martyrdom of the Goddess Hypatia	EY 1438	CE 416
Life-dates of Leonardo da Vinci	EY 2474 - 2541	CE 1452 – 1519
	EY 5.1022	1 BCE
	EY 5.1023	CE 1
Martyrdom of the Divine Cicero	EY 5.0980.XIII.12	December 7, 43 BCE
U.S. Declaration of Independence	EY 5.2798.VII.26	July 4, 1776 CE
Bastille Day	EY 5.2811.VIII.8	July 14, 1789 CE
Texas Declaration of Independence	EY 5.2858.III.14	March 2, 1836 CE
Kristallnacht in Nazi Germany	EY 5.2960.XII.13	November 9, 1938 CE
Japanese attack on Pearl Harbor	EY 5.2963.XIII.13	December 7, 1941 CE
First Lunar Landing	EY 5.2991.VIII.13	July 20, 1969 CE
Revelation of *The Danaa*	EY 5.3000.VII.13	June 22, 1978 CE

Standard and colloquial Danaan date notations:

EY 5.2991.XIII.13	=	13 Holly 2991	=	13/8/91
EY 5.2798.VII.25	=	25 Oak 2798	=	25/7/98
EY 5.3005.Y	=	Yevoa, 3005	=	Y/05
EY 5.3002.A	=	Anisosa, 3002	=	A/02

bloody proselytizing of the peoples of Northern Europe. This tradition began because of a superstitious refusal to use the Hebrew/Indo-european name of their deity: יהוה—*Yava*, also rendered as **Yahweh**, who is ***Iove*** [yō´-vɛ] (*Jupiter: Iovi-pater* "Father Yoveh", *that is*, "Father Jehovah") of the Romans and ***Dyava*** of the Vedic Aryans. Rather than re-use the old name, missionaries to the Germanic peoples sanctified a general term for deity, in an attempt to make a tribal sky-god into a universal overlord, and to hide the fact that their deity was the same concept as a "pagan" deity they had discredited.

This infringement on our rights is just one example of the paranoid schizophrenia of the Idolatrous Abrahamists, who scream for religious freedom in one instance and destroy that same freedom in another, like the indigenous-culture-obliterating missionaries and mullahs. They continue to be like the Puritans, who fled to the American continent for relief from religious persecution, yet denied freedom of religion to any who were not numbered among "the saints", as they themselves deemed to tally them. All this has had but one effect: the deepening of their mental illness—witch hunts, inquisitions and massacres.

If a Danaan is forced to use money with the "motto" on it, it does not mean that the Danaan believes the motto or puts any store by it. We must use the currency of the realm, even though it be the tool of tyranny religious.

If a Danaan is forced to swear using the other phrase, that oath is only so binding as the Danaan individually decides it to be. It is a violation of our rights and, therefore, invalidates anything it tries to force upon us.

This statutory destruction of constitutionally guaranteed rights has, since the phrases' first mandated usage, made the governments of the United States insolvent by breach of their *Contract of Governance*.

This has not, however, reduced the strength or the validity of the Constitution of the United States, nor the love and dedication of the American Danaans to it and to the Declaration of Independence.

Our loyalty is steadfast: our anger at this religious tyranny is growing. We will not flee to Rhode Island with the dissenters of old. We will stand up for the Constitution and the freedom it guarantees.

⸙4 It is another common symptom of the state of paranoid schizophrenia of the Three Great Fallacies, that these fallacies ascribe "Oedipal" complexes to other peoples, yet cannot see it where it truly exists: in themselves. This arises from an inability to look at their own beliefs and myths with a discerning eye, and is abetted by a mistaken idea of what an Oedipal complex truly is.

An Oedipal complex is a self-doubting, self-deprecating, self-negating dependency on an external authority figure. The classical Freudian examples and theories revealed only the parent of the opposite sex of the person under observation as the authority figure. The use of the name *Oedipus* also seemed to say that the condition was limited to males. This misinterpretation of data also led to foolish, erroneous hypotheses about the nature of homosexuality.

The authority figure involved does not have to be the parent of the opposite sex. It does not have to be the one of the opposite sex, or one of the parents, *or* even a living human being! Oedipal complexes can be brought on by any of a multitude of different psychological traumas, from child abuse to drug abuse to inherent organic dysfunction. This is why so many drug-freaks turn into Jesus-freaks after their drug abuse has diminished their mental and emotional powers and they go through what is commonly called *burn-out*. The controlling, manipulating, drug abuse to which they had previously surrendered is replaced by neurotic capitulation to the abusing control of "the Lord" and his deputies.

The self-replacing, dominant personality can be one person, a group of people, chemicals, or concepts which deny the individual full and free expression of that individual's personality.

It is in this way that the sociopathic leaders of Idolatrous Abrahamism have enforced control over Woman, "source of all sin and suffering": uneducated, unenfranchised, underpaid: the breeding tool of the *divine-imaged* sex.

📣5   It was in a fit of Oedipal mania that Christians killed one of the most distinguished of the Danaan Martyrs, a lady of Alexandria, Egypt. Hypatia by name, She is now in Unity with Our Lady: a porpoise-soul swimming joyfully in the Universal Sea of Athena's Love. We call this great woman the Goddess Hypatia—the Goddess revealed in the Life Hypatia, now having returned to the River of Life.

Born in EY 1393, our Hypatia had grown into a beautiful woman, full of grace, pietas and high intelligence. Never having been married, She was singularly dedicated to Her work as head librarian of the largest of libraries that existed before the 30th century—the Great Library of Alexandria—and to Her research in and writings on the science of Mathematics.

Because of Her beauty, Her refusal to heed the breeding commands and other doctrines of the upstart Hebræo-christianist bishop of Alexandria, Cyril, and because of Her unflinching dedication to the search for knowledge, that same "shepherd" Cyril, caring father of the lost, minister of the downtrodden, feeder of lambs, incited the Nitrian monks and a mob of his followers against Her. In EY 1438, as She was walking to the Library, She was attacked on the street. These Men of God stripped Her, abused Her, then in a blasphemous use of the products of Her Mother, the Sea, they flayed the still-living, sacred flesh from Her body with abalone shells. After dragging the bloody pieces of Her corpse to the Library, they set fire to the building, thereby annihilating Her body and, at the same time, destroying the single largest collection of that which Idolatrous Abrahamists hate and from which they have the most to fear:

knowledge. Such was the first of the book-burnings they have become so fond of.

This is not the first example one could pull from the pages of human history of the maliciousness of the ignorant and their leaders. But it is one of the most heinous that occurred before the Inquisition, the St Bartholomew's Day Massacre and the Annihilation of the European Jews. They are damned for their blood-thirstiness: having incited, permitted, and inflicted the Holocaust is the death knell of traditional Christianity. ***Sanguis in manibus Jovis: et quisnam nunc Jehovem servaret?*** — *Blood on the hands of Jove, and who now may save Jehovah?*

According to Hebræo-christianist mythology, there have been humans who lived previous to the sudden appearance of and outside of "grace"—they were not part of the Body of the Elect: they lived before or too far removed from damnation-proselytization. Therefore their fates were sealed by that *all-powerful, omnipresent* deity, that is, by the fable-writer who invented the oven-fire called Hell. The Great White Father who chose the few, and rejected all others, invented both the mechanism of Auschwitz and the "justification" for its use.

Here is a *father* who chooses to eradicate painfully the multitude of non-believers, even though he is supposed to be *their* father, too: *it is indeed a perverted religion in which the father forces his 'children' to beg him not to torture and destroy them!* — ***sanctified child abuse***. It is the Christians who celebrate a festival day by praying, "O Almighty God, who ... madest infants to glorify thee by their deaths ...". Those infants, of course, were Jewish.

Death & Hell is the fablist's solution to "the Pagan Problem". The Nazi atrocities were not the first time patriarchists have found justification for genocide. Nor was it the first time the christianists have found in their scriptures justification for murdering Jews, women, pagans, blacks, wiccans, homosexuals, or anyone possessing land, property or power they desired.

Unlike Idolatrous Abrahamist mythology, there was no sudden, limited epiphany of the Goddess: we realized Her presence those 50,000 years ago as gracefully as one now feels the approach of a warming dawn after a long, cold night. She has been with all humanity always: around, within and throughout human life.

It is man who has lost sight of Her! It has been the greed and the power-thrusts of the bearers of the iron sword, the warrior-priests, who have tried to make humanity forget the Truth: to worship them, the god they fabricated in their image and their blood-dripping volume of fables. **For their Bible is *Mein Kampf* and free humanity is its *Jew*.**

A noted British physician, actor and director has asserted that the "great" religions (by which he means the sky-god, father-god religions) have attained their "greatness" because of an ability to get one out of oneself, to sublimate, almost to destroy self in *other-identitiness, other-worldliness*. But loss of self is not a sign of greatness, it is a symptom of schizophrenia: of the mob-behavior of the Alexandrians, lynch-mob Southerners, Soviet secret-police, and the Nazi *Brown Shirts*. Indeed, paranoid schizophrenia is the predominant condition of the adherents of these religions, all of which were founded on the sword and have been preserved by the unrestrained, *sanctified* use of it.

It is not in the destruction of Self, but in Self-realization, Universe-realization and Interrelationship-realization—knowledge of oneself, of the true nature of the world we live in and of how all things work together—that true greatness resides. In ignoring their selves, their true natures, the people involved in these so-called great religions have lost contact with reality: they live on a flat world in the center of a static universe—they learn about the past, but do not believe in it. They believe only those fictions allegedly written long ago, as if their assumed antiqueness verified and sanctified them. They do not know what the Universe truly is.

Self-delusion is not the way of the Universe. Those who do not understand the truth of their situation will be destroyed by it.

⛋6   Every particle, of whatever absolute size, has its resonance, its own cyclical, periodic properties which establish its identity, as well as its resonant-interaction properties with any other particle or group of particles with which it may interact. This resonance is the sum and synergy of all properties and characteristics of the particle.

Each living being has its own resonance, produced by the sum and synergy of every particle of which it is composed.

These resonances, this universal cycularity which exists in everything from the smallest particle to the very Universe itself, is that which we term its *kami* [神], or its *cosmosalos* [κόσμος + σάλος]: *the moving to and fro of the Universe*. It is because of the kami of hydrogen and oxygen atoms (and the kami of their constituent particles) that the kami of water is such as it is: the interaction of their resonances, their cycularities, produces a resonance that is *water*, with all its unique properties: its *kami*, its *cosmosalos*.

Something's kami is its "being-ness", its identity in the widest definition imaginable.

It is the cosmosalos which demands that we live in accord with our true inner nature as humans and our true identity as individuals, members of and parts of the higher orders of the kami which are the Universe.

The influence of the cosmosalos is felt through its mysterious power of creating, delineating and harmonizing, called 結び *musubi* or *synapteia* [συνάπτεια: *connection*]. The way of the kami is 誠 *makoto* or *aletheia* [ἀλήθεια: *truth*]. Unity with the kami is pietas: *alethicardia* or 真心 *magokoro* [ἀλήθεια + καρδία: *a heart of truth*: 誠の心 *makoto no kokoro*]. The kami is the incarnation of the Prime Imperative.

In realizing the kami, we gain an appreciation for the beauty and awesomeness of Nature: of divine Creativity. For the Divine is a living presence, dynamic, revealed in many guises, many forms, experiencing constant transformation.

The kami is the divine inner-mystery. It unifies through the revelation of separateness-interconnected, of differences-deeply interrelated: of the common-story-identical, distinct in every retelling.

Amaterasu and Selene are One in Radiance. The Sun and the Moon are the same Brilliance, for all are Athena, All-Understanding.

⛤7 The great River of Life is the Universe. Each thing is a part of that river, flowing through all things. It imbues each living creature with that divine creating and harmonizing power, the core of existence: *the Goddess Within*. All creatures possess a nature that is divine—the way of the Prime Imperative, the heart of truth, bright, pure, serene. It is in rejecting the solid foundation of the Divine that mankind has gotten into horrible states of psychological imbalance, adopting unnatural attitudes of pessimism, fear and disregard of his fellow creatures' rights. This species imperialism is the reason so many have been killed in the name of the father-gods, why slavery ever existed, why the whales are in danger of extinction. The hyperaneric refuse to see themselves as anything less than the lords of men and nature. They do not feel the life-power surging through them. They do not feel their hearts' pumping sea-water through their veins. They do not feel the Cosmos still expanding, the stars pulsing, the tree still living in the wood of the desk which is their command-center.

Life is ever-present, ever-changing, ever-renewing. It cannot be destroyed. It is the Mother of the Universe.

Life-forms, however, are delicate. When one life-form vanishes, all the living are robbed of the beauty of its Being, of the joy of sharing its existence. Therefore, even though Life is ever-present, we cherish its every individual, its every form, for in those forms we find kinship in the Divine. The tree is my brother; the butterfly, my sister; the porpoise, my other self.

Respect for the fragility and importance of the individual life is the first step toward immortality.

As Our Goddess cherishes each one of us, so do we love every life. Athena still weeps for the dead of Marathon, the families of Lidice, the children of Hiroshima and Nagasaki. We must not let them be forgotten. These souls are still with us, urging us from the Great River to protect Life: to assume our true place as Guardians of the Creatures and their Liberties.

The highest purpose of the human species is to justify having received the Gift of Life, by loving all Life.

⛢8 In the seventh section of my first letter, I mentioned the three aspects of species development. These three are the development of a species' mental powers from being (1) a participative species, to being (2) an observant species as well; thence into (3) a guardian species. As progress is made through these, the former aspect or aspects are not discarded, but are built upon. In human life, these aspects are paralleled by the developmental stages of childhood, adolescence and adulthood.

The sixth myriadæon of human culture and humanity's observational period began at the time of the final onslaughts of the hyperaneric warrior-priests against the People of the Goddess. The next three millennia were marked by these priests' continuous struggle to obliterate all devotion to Our Lady throughout the world, until they have, of late, become willing to destroy the Earth in a desperate attempt to force their "messiah" to return.

Bloody though their efforts have been, they have failed miserably. We have won the victory for our species through love of Liberty and Learning. The greatest accomplishments of this dark age are ours—even our edifices are the glory of the world: the Parthenon, Our Lady's Cathedral of Chartres, Notre Dame de Paris, the Statue of Liberty, the Palace of Westminster, the Capitol of the Texas Republic, the sun-brilliant University Tower and the fog-draped Campanile.

Humanity is now entering its guardian-species aspect. It is we, the Danaans, who are leading the way. For it is in this period that true Love of all living things arises, along with the desire and ability to protect that Life through drawing on our knowledge, intuition and reason to guide ourselves, our actions and tools, and our myriad hosts of cousin life-forms forward into a future of Love, Care and Respect—of sharing the Joy of being alive.

The Goddess's Love for Her Creatures truly resonates throughout the Universe.

⛧9 My Phædra, if in this letter I have sounded bitter and angry, you know that this anger is not directed at the great masses of people who have had nothing but the old gods to cling to. The Goddess treats them with love and consideration because of the Love they can show for each other.

Some would say that I should not condemn a set of beliefs merely because of the heinous acts of certain of their adherents. I say I can, nay, **must** condemn any tenets which will allow heinous acts to occur. For if they in any way permit, prompt or condone those barbarities, those beliefs are as guilty of commission of those acts as is anyone who took direct part. **The creed that lives by the sword is stained each time the sword swings.**

Any deity whose establishment as a deity requires the slaughter of human beings or human rights is damned by his own requirements. Such god-concepts are to be loathed and reviled: they reduce their beguiled believers to a level beneath that of the lowly slime-mold. For at least the slime-mold has its liberty and lives at one with the Universe.

"...they put everyone to the sword, male and female, young and old...", yet **"...all the silver and gold...is sacred...to Yava..."** Someone must stand up for all the "Children of Palestine," for the rights of free Humanity.

Too many creeds assert that humanity is born to suffer, in "sin", that such is our basic nature. For these creeds the only escape from this condition of suffering is self-annihilation in the release from individuality through attainment of *nirvana* or *grace*.

Yet to destroy the individual is to do away with the basic unit of Life. To obliterate the individual is to destroy the balance of Nature: an attempt to impose human misunderstanding on Natural Law. This is a disease of modern civilizations, both Eastern and Western. It is their perpetuation of this cavalier disregard of Nature that will destroy the Earth—if we permit it.

It is We who have the remedy for this condition. It is we who will build a new Civilization, uniting all peoples in Love of Life, Liberty and Peace.

Yet, I have my anger, still. For it is pointed and direct: I am incensed at the leaders of the usurper religions, who continue to bilk the common people, who continue to spew forth lies, who continue to enslave the minds of the people with vacuous nonsense just so these "pastors" can continue to fleece their flocks as closely as possible, to get as much cash out of them as they can.

It is them I despise, for they first despised the Goddess and the Liberty of Her People. It is they who would enslave all nations, who would destroy the Earth utterly. It is they who think life is their trophy for having "conquered" nature, rather than realizing that **Life is the Gift of Nature**: the dowry of the Virgin Mother Goddess, inexhaustible in Her fertilizing power, mysteriously renewed at the Source of Cosmic Life—renewing the Source at the same instant. She is the Gate of All Mysteries.

MY PHÆDRA, WE are the new Civilization: building a new world of human potential at the very Gate of the Universe...

> ATHENA, Goddess, Great and True,
> Sister, Mother and Dame, no few,
> Builder of Cities, Creator, to You
> This song will I sing, and another one, too.

OCVLIS·APERTIS
CORDE·SPERANTE
MENTE·EXPLORANTE
VISV·MIRABILE·STAT·VERITAS

ATHENADORVS·HERACLES·PHÆDRÆ·PROTOGONIÆ·S·D·

EY 5.3005.IX.1
CHRYSOPYLÆ·HESPERIDIVM·HORTO

MOST WORTHY PHÆDRA, GREAT Distance often serves more to unite than to divide. So I hope may our separation continue to provide impetus for maintaining strong channels of communication. Although this is the last of this set of three letters, I have much more to gather, organize, reveal; so much more to give to you, to our Danaan sisters and brothers, to the Goddess. There are so very many lives who need hope, so many chains to be broken, so much joy to be shared.

⸘1 My Phædra, from time to time questions arise about the Greek and Roman mythologies: why we use names found in them, what relationship they bear to our teachings, what store we put in them. The bewilderment you mention at the strangeness, the seeming incoherency and duplicitousness of that body of myth is very understandable.

I will explain all this, but first I would point out that the Greek myths and the oldest Hebrew mythology were being codified at approximately the same time: at around the beginning of the [4,600,0]51st millennium. The Roman revision and expansion of the Greek myths, and the Christian redaction and inflation of the Hebrew myths were going on just after the start of the 52nd millennium. However, we must go back farther into the past to see the entire story of the development of these four interrelated groups of fables, back to the earliest of the Indo-european peoples.

The Kurgans were the first Indo-europeans of whom we have record. These Kurgan peoples began the infiltration of our settlements, our villages—what is now referred to as the *Old Europe* Civilization—during the 47th millennium, forcefully introducing male deities and patriarchal barbarities: human sacrifice, slavery, genocide. Later, the descendants of the Kurgans, the Indo-european war-bands, became the wandering, horse-riding pirates of the Steppes. In certain areas of the Goddess-born civilizations which had arisen in the 48th and 49th millennia, the patriarchal warrior-priests were extremely successful in destroying the social system that had just engendered Civilization itself. They were remorseless in their use of violence and so gained the upper hand, for the peaceful people of the Earth often realize too late the danger they face and how much they need a strong, active defense.

So it happened to the peoples who were invaded by these Aryan war-parties: the Luvi (*Levites*), the Mitanni, the Persians, the Brahmins. Because of their sudden, merciless and continued onslaught, almost all historical traces of Goddess Devotion were obliterated in those regions.

In Greece, however, the waves of conquest were slower, less vicious, farther separated in time, and therefore less effective at suppressing the natural religion of the native peoples: their love for the Great Goddess. A series of social compromises, varying from location to location, arose from the struggles between the bands of warriors and the resentful Goddess-worshipping Pelasgians. This was when the patriarchists made the Goddess in Her Myriad Names into, first, the mothers of the patriarchal deities, then their sisters, then the subordinate wives and children of those deities.

The Six Goddess epithets and the six male godkins formed the heavenly court of the sky-god, Di^{w}os, Dyava, Iove (*"Jove"*), who ruled from the mountaintop, rumbling in the clouds and throwing out thunder-bolts, just like that same god, who, as

יהוה—Iovë/Yava—in the clouds on his mountain, rumbled and belched fire and smoke columns to frighten the "Israelites" into submission. (One of the early names of this deity is *Elohim*: אלהים. *Elohim* is cognate with the English word *volcano*, for it is ultimately an Indo-european word, found as ᶠελχανομ [*welkhanom*] in Ancient Greek, suspiciously close to the Sanskrit भल्लखनम् [*bhallakhanam*]. This means *dart-thrower* or *projectile-mouth*, a very good name for a volcano god! This is the god of Mt Ararat, the only active volcanic peak in the Middle East.)

These blood-drawn compromises were encoded among the people who came to be speakers of Classical Greek through the invention of patriarchal myths to accompany the pictures of the sacred rites of the Goddess, as these rites had survived through the Kurgan and Dorian debasement. This procedure of creative writing, called *iconotropism*, is why the classical Greek Myths are such a mixed up, violent, confusing tangle. They are the few surviving threads of the Aryan sky-god, thunder-god mythology, woven into a larger collection of stories fleshing out the icons showing individual, area-specific traditions of the Goddess-worshipping peoples. These names and ceremonies, gathered from a large region of Europe and Asia Minor over a long period of time, were culticly, purposely misinterpreted in an attempt to weaken devotion to the Goddess in favor of the male gods.

As codified by Hesiod and by the Homeric writers, the obvious, common thread running through these myths is the domination of woman, represented in the numerous epithets of the Goddess, a mastery to be exercised by warrior-man and the male gods he had made in his image. Though not as blatant, nor so heinous as in Idolatrous Abrahamist fable, this domination is just as pervasive and persistent in these stories.

We use the names of the Goddess found in the Greek and Roman myths as ours because they were ours first. We do not believe in those myths any more than we believe in the Idolatrous Abrahamist fairy tales: those fables are both sets of political, social, economic propaganda, established and imposed in order to deprive part of the human race of their rights as free-born individuals.

Of all the names by which the Danaans invoked the Goddess at that time, one name, one Realization, was too strong to allow even the Dorians to make Her into the mythic sister/lover/wife of Joveh. She was so important that She had to be intimately associated only with Joveh—She could not be arbitrarily assigned a mother, for, as Mother of the Universe, there would have been no logic to such an arrangement. The mythographers had to invent a story that She was born directly from the body of their supreme male god, no matter how unnatural the process.

But Athena did not sprout from the scalp of some cloud-demon. She is the Eternal One, Mother of All Living, the All-Wisdom. For the same mythographers who came up with the ludicrous story of Her birth from Jove's head had to admit that all their deities—even Jove himself—went to Her for advice and counsel: they always needed Her help to be able to achieve success.

How Her form shines when you strip away the lies of the patristics! For She is the Spirit of Universal-Existence, transcending all Ages, all Potentialities. She is the All-Harmony.

⸸2 So many of the patristic lords say that society's ills would be cured if everyone would just "turn to Jee-zuss". But today's social problems do not stem from not *accepting* Jove/Jehovah, or from not "surrendering" to Islam. These ailments exist because the social system imposed by Idolatrous Abrahamism does not work. Any system which destroys psychological independence, initiative and growth and which uses negative commands, curses and damnations to achieve control carries within that negative-imperialism the cause of its own failure and destruction: sanctified sexism, slavery, genocide. To expect a system built on violence to bring forth peace is high folly—*for they have planted putrid flesh in their desert, yet wait for peaches and flowers to appear*. A tree with rotten heartwood is a rotten tree. The root of Idolatrous Abrahamism is the tyranny of hell-fire terrorism.

Patriarchists are fond of killing, as they think it makes them lords of life and death. In reality, it only makes them murderers.

A deity cannot bear the images of compassion and hatred at the same time. He cannot be both napalmer *and* nurse, for being the former belies being the latter. The murderer in benevolent mask is murderer still. The psychology of patriarchy, primitive, dictatorial, demands that the "will" of the Father be enforced, no matter what the cost in human life: for the ability to kill non-believers has become biblical "proof" of the "power and goodness of God" and the "power of the will of God".

Our world is tottering on the brink of destruction, destabilized by macho male patriarchists wasting the wealth of the nations, building more and more bombs, driven by the need to protect their power-base. We must deflate these swaggering fools and begin the reorientation of world society to engender the peace of the global village.

We need leaders who have learned and fostered balanced values. We need leaders who are not driven by hyperaneric neuroses, but who have learned the lesson of the Prime Imperative: who have achieved wholeness of view and compassion of heart. We need leaders who have tapped their own wells of mother-values. The lion will fight to grab a meal, to protect his domination of the pride, will kill the cubs of a former ruler of the pride. The lioness hunts to provide food for her cubs, her sisters and herself.

The fostering of mother-values is not limited to genetic females, nor is its banishment exclusively male. Anyone can develop these qualities if he or she wishes to be able to love deeply, protectively yet unclingingly.

The Danaan name for this treasure is *tecnoteria*: *guardianship of that which has been born*. Male or female can be *tecnóterous*—the bearer of a deep and abiding love for the humans and other creatures who cohabit this Earth.

It is tecnoteria when we learn to love so much that we are

able to overcome selfishness and jealousy, to love others so fully that for them to live, and to live free and true to their inner selves is our greatest desire: to love without prejudice or possessiveness, on a personal, societal and species basis.

It is the person who has attained tecnoteria who is the greatest asset to the continuation of the human species, to the continuation of life itself: for it is that person who loves others enough to **let them be free**. Respect for the fragility and importance of the individual life as part of the Universal Life is the first step toward tecnoteria, the first step toward immortality.

Tecnoteria, mother-value, is dedication to life and liberty, to the growth of knowledge and wisdom in the children, along with commitment to protect that life, liberty and the bright future of those infants. It is the value-set of the springbok when she charges the hyenas to keep them from her fawn. It is the values of the mockingbird, dive-bombing the family cat to keep it away from her nest. Yet the mockingbird does not cringe from teaching her young to fly: to establish their individual identities; to exercise their freedom of the skies.

The springbok and the mockingbird take from other creatures the substances to prolong their lives and the lives of their offspring, as established in the free marketplace of survival. They do not kill wantonly, murder others of their species or other species merely to satisfy greed or to "prove" a point of some vapid theology.

The grass of the field does not despise the lumbering ox; the zebra does not hate the hunting lioness; nor does the hare revile the soaring eagle. The life that is prey gives life to the predator. The predator in turn is prey for other predators, bestowing life to life; death is but a passage, a marker of change—an end and beginning in the same instant.

In struggling for the preservation of all life, we need not fear individual death. We may dread its associated pain and discomfort. We might worry that we have not accomplished all we would like to have done before our passing through. We may be concerned for the welfare of those we will leave behind.

But in Unity with the Goddess, all fears and worries melt away. All things share the sacred One-ness of the All-Mother, Source of Love and Liberty, Athena, Greatest and Best.

⚷3   In a dream, I was walking with our Athena along the shore of the Lake, in the warmth of a spring afternoon, beneath the deep-endless blue sky. I asked Her to reveal Her laws to me, so that I might learn Her Truth by heart, hold it ever in my mind and practice it in Life.

She said, "I will write the Law for you, My son. However, My Truth lies not in what is written, but in the writing—not in the reading, but in the realization of having read." She then took Her willow staff and, with the end, made this shape on the gently rippling surface of the Lake: α.

"This is the letter *alpha*," She said, "which was both the first letter and the numeral *one* of the Danaan Greeks. The water holds the Law, but does not restrain it. The Law is within the water; the Law is outside of the water. The Law is the water; the water is the Law. Yet the water is water, still. This is my Law, my Eternal Truth. You need only open your inner eyes, unmask your innermost ears. Your Inner Self, your Goddess Within, whispers it in your every breath: your heart has always known the Law."

When I awoke, it was the deep middle of the night. The full moon kept shimmering sentinel in the clear wind, shivering in across the Bay. I could not fathom the meaning of the divine metaphor. Try as I might, I could not find the mystical key. Then the great calm arose within me; serenity came as I surrendered the sky to the uplifting Moon.

It was then that I beheld how Her staff had skimmed across the Lake's sun-dappled waves. I saw water, Mother of Life, behaving as water always will: all things are true to their inner nature. Each thing's inner self and outer self, working together, produce the Self Complete—the Unity that is the consistent, harmonious Eternal Truth: the Synergy of the Kami.

Every thing true to its inner reality becomes the fertile Valley of Universal delight, fulfillment and peace.

The *numeral*-alpha stands for the Prime Imperative, the First Law of All Living: resonance in harmony with the All-Resonance. The *letter*-alpha is the first letter of Her Name, the Name of the All-Name, of Her upon whom galaxies hang dependent, yet is Herself the very Font of Liberty.

The *letter*-alpha is also the first letter of the word ἄνθρωπος *anthropos*, "humanity": for he is the only animal that has done so much to destroy his inner being, has done so much contrary to the Prime Imperative, and yet, can still be its most blessèd expression.

Some laws are carved into stone. But stone does not adapt, does not adjust, does not live. Stone merely crumbles and melts away.

Her Law is written on water, of water, within water. It will never pass away.

Her Law is the very substance of the Universe.

⇥4 There will be times in Danaans' lives when we will feel sad, perplexed, confused. Sadness comes with the loss of cherished lives, of pets, friends, mates: when we lose those who are dear to us and with whom we have shared our lives. This is natural: the mother fur seal cries in the snow for its child just clubbed, the cow bawls for the calf taken away, elephants mourn over the bleached bones of their fallen comrades. We grow strong in sharing our sorrows, as we do in sharing our joys. Comfort the bereaved—do not ask them not to cry: it is the heart without love that does not feel sorrow.

We will sometimes be perplexed and confused because of the actions of non-Danaans: for many can naught but run scared. No animal is more dangerous than when it is frightened or feels threatened; and no animal is more dangerous at any time than is man.

But take heart, be strong to defend yourselves; be agile. Pool your skills, abilities and your contributions to build a better world for yourselves, your fellow Danaans and your cousin clans. Rejoice in sharing the achievements of life, in the Five Transits, in the Conubia and in the Community of the Waters. The strengths of the Danaan people is in the individual, aggregate and synergistic strengths of each of us.

Remember the victory of our ancient Athenian brothers who, despite tremendous odds, at Marathon defeated their great enemy, the man who called himself "King of Kings and Lord of Lords". Do not despair of the attacks of the paranoid, the ranting of the ignorant, the phantom brimstone of the patriarch's profiting prophets. Remember how Athena raised up Her City and saved Greek Liberty from Aryan tyranny.

She is always with those who live in love for Her, Her People and their Liberty.

⸙5 The full moon was rising above the farmlands in the east as the summer solstice-sun's setting rays made riot with colors incomparable above the hills of the west, far across the mountain-girding ribbon of glinting water. I found myself at the summit of the Mountain, in a grove of five trees: a Birch, Willow, Hawthorn, Oak and Elder, all of which bowed in the wind to the single Olive tree, removed, unstirred.

Suddenly, above the Olive, the Goddess appeared, towering over me in great inverted triangles of light, whose apexes were within my chest: it was as if the Great Radiance shone out from within me, yet as if it flowed down from somewhere out in the Universe, and its rays converged within me. It was as if the Great Radiance was a separate existence, holding all the Universe in itself, and me within that: all images swirling among each other.

Then, in front of the Olive appeared a crystalline table and before it the Lady became the Three-Who-are-the-One: Persephone, Demeter, Hera: Maiden, Mother, Grandmother.

They were constantly changing, unceasingly constant. They called themselves the *Danaids*: Linda, Cameira, Ialysa.

In an instant, one had become Lindäus, one Cameira, the other Ialysus. Then, one appeared as Lindus, another Cameiräus, the other now Ialysa: thence Linda again, but with Cameirus and Ialysäus, transcending gender-aspects, all united in mother-value, in *tecnoteria*, in *pietas*, in love of the Prime Imperative. They were the Universal matrix, changing from intersection to intersection of the flow of the Great Eternal, revealing the interconnectedness of all things. Each was Three, and so they were Nine, yet they were Three and All were the One: all radiant within the All-Radiance—the Infinity of the Thirteen—the One, the Three, the Nine.

In the brilliance I saw the animal spirits approach the Holiness. Some carried long ears of wheat, some figs, others scallop shells. Most, however, brought only themselves to Our Lady. The first to reach Her, was a group of three: a fur seal pup, a young humpback whale and a sea otter pup. These sea mammals, marian children, had been sacrificed to human vanity and stupidity.

The young otter dove down as if into the deep sea, and popping up with an abalone shell, floated on its back, chirping among the spirit waves. With a bright bark, it picked the shell up off its stomach and held it out in its small paws, offering it to the Goddess.

The Danaid Cameiräus received it, and, facing the spirits, held it high for all to see, saying

Vita e Vita, per Vitam,	*Life from Life, through Life,*
in Vitam.	*into Life.*
Benedicta es,	*Blessed are You,*
Athanat' Athenaia.	*Immortal Athena.*
Terbenedicti estis,	*Thrice blessed are you,*
Vitæ creaturæ,	*Creatures of Life,*
Liberi Æternæ Matris.	*Children of the Eternal Mother*
Novies benedicta es,	*Ninetimes blessed are You,*
Dea Magna,	*Great Goddess,*
Amaterasu Candida,	*Bright Amaterasu,*
Infinitus Amor.	*Infinite Love*

Then the Three turned toward the One, bowed as they clapped thrice and together chanted

Benedicta es,	*Blessed are You,*
Athena, Mater Nostra,	*Athena, Our Mother,*
Quoniam nobis Vitam,	*For that to us our life,*
Vim Amoris,	*Strength of Love,*
Scientiamque	*And Knowledge*
Dona dedisti.	*You gave us as gifts.*
Spiritus Sancta,	*Sacred Spirit,*
Duc nos ad Te.	*Lead us to You.*
Alethōs.	*In truth.*

In a flash of golden light, I had become the Goddess's dove, flying high above the ceremony of adoration, hearing the sonorous words, the deep-resounding melodies of voices and organs of music, the pulsing love of the creature world. The Danaids and the animal spirits chanted, sang and meditated, preparing themselves for the Unity with Athena.

As I soared, the Goddess lifted me up ever higher, to open the Cosmos, to make all holy things known, to reveal the Union of the sacred words.

I saw the Danaids draw sparkling water in earthen vessels from the sacred spring, the Source of Cosmic Life. Thrice they blessed the triune water, then Lindäus poured water into the abalone shell held by Ialysus as Cameira blessed it with holy words and the *trigonos* sign. As Ialysäus held the shell to the sea otter's mouth so that the pup might drink, Ialysa said the *cantio*:

Vita divina,	*Divine Life,*
Deā sis una!	*Be one with the Goddess!*

to which the pup barked "Alethōs".

Ialysus wiped the shell with linen pure; Lindäus poured more water from the vessel into the shell; Cameira blessed it. Ialysa handed the shell to the sea otter baby, who held it to the mouth of the whale and said the cantio to her great brother.

After this, the shell was again cleaned, filled, blessed. Ialysäus held it to the white fur seal's mouth for the whale, as the huge young whale softly sang the cantio to his small cousin.

Thus it transpired: one creature ministering to the next, who then turned and served the one coming after, bestowing the blessing of the Goddess—Life and Love for all living things. Life flowing resplendent from one Living to the Next.

When all the creatures had partaken of the water, the last creature ministered to the first Danaid, then the Danaids served one another. All the remaining water was poured, a libation to the comfort of Mother Earth, while all the spirits joined with the Danaids in chanting the Benediction of the Earth. As the myriad voices rose in wave upon wave of melody, the Radiance became so overwhelming as I was lofted on surf-pounding, supernovas' all-consuming tidal waves!

Suddenly, I was alone atop the Mountain. The City's lights glistened against the cool night, almost day from the shine of the high-vaulting Moon. I could still hear Cameira's last phrase as the vision faded:

Ite in Vita, Diæcuri!	*Go within Life, Generations of the Goddess!*
Alethōs	*In Truth!*

I was shivering cold and burning hot: there was ice in my hair and sweat on my brow. And paradise deep within.

Lead Her People back from the Battlefield! Show them the cool, blue-green meadows of Love. Restore the marbled halls of the Temple of Peace Victorious.

⸙6 In the vision on the mountaintop, Athena showed us how She delights in the congregation of Her People, for there they join together, strengthening the bonds of all living things in love, knowledge and peace. She made plain how, in drawing on our individual strengths to show compassion to others, our own compassion is increased, as well as the compassionate vitality of our community.

She revealed how freedom within organization gives orderly expression to the fulfillment of human mental, physical and spiritual needs. Thus She gives us Her special devotees, the Danaids, the leaders of the Danaans in our communal service, the *triodos*: the unity at the meeting of the three roads, the three paths. Young, middle-aged, old; female, laotrophic, male; the Danaids are Athena Promachos, Athena the Champion. For the Danaids are not mere priests and priestesses—old, sexist terms, remnants of an ignoble, murderous, fire-altar aryan past. They are the guides, the teachers, the synthesizers: combining the parts so as to reveal the Whole, the Unity of the Goddess, in leading the people in their Joy—celebrating the ceremonies of ritual union between humanity and the Universe.

So, we who stand before our beloved people, chanting in Greek, Latin and the Vernaculars, dressed in shining Hypatian togas, honor Athena: Danu and Her People. For we do not rave, declaiming what humans must do to avert imagined divine anger, nor do we feverishly command them to live exactly as we might chose to live, nor according to some specious *preordained* plan.

We are the destroyers of limitations, the broadeners of horizons, the openers of long-forgotten pastures.

We lead the Danaans to the border of the Universe, point out over the ever-evolving Cosmos to say, "The future is yours. And we are ever with you."

¶7 My Phædra, these visions, these insights, these grand vistas are worth little if the individual cannot internalize their essence, recreate them in the individual's own inner life.

We each find our own inner myths, our stories of great power that lead us to the desire for and understanding of the Goddess. We cannot package Goddess-devotion and sell it like instant soup, prayer cloths or indulgences. Nor can we give commandments that one must obey in order to attain Her Realization: each person has the path within—it is there awaiting discovery and use. We cannot walk that path for others—they each must make their own odysseys if they would know the infinity of human possibility that is Athena.

We can, however, share our experiences, our ways of reaching that Understanding. And it is vital that we venerate and share each other's joy in attaining that Unity, in celebrating the triodos, as well as in caring for each other in everyday life.

We share the intimate ecstasy of our continuous individual discovery, our community dedication and our part in bringing about the infinity of the possible for all living things.

MY PHÆDRA, IN This human village called the Earth, it is love of the Earth that will preserve the life of our village. It is when each of us realizes this is the only village, this is our only home, this is very nearly our last chance to revive love for this planet among humans, that we will find that true commitment to Life, Peace and Justice that will carry us forward into a bright future of Human Life.

> ATHENA, Goddess, Great and True,
> Sister, Mother and Dame, no few,
> Builder of Cities, Creator, to You
> This song will I sing, and all other ones, too.

大門道
TA·MEN·TAO
The·Tao·of·Athenadorus

TA MEN TAO
THE TAO OF ATHENADORUS

Danaan Press

EY 5.3006 - 5.3039

Ēdidit diē EY 5. 3039.VIII.01

INTRODUCTION

This book, the *Ta Men Tao*, is an expanded restatement, re-interpretation of the *Tao Te Ching* attributed to the quasi-mythical Lao Tzu.

My expansion and restatement is not a literal translation in the scholarly sense: it has been cast in a specifically more poetic way, while bringing forth and fleshing out more fully the Danaan aspects underpinning this great work, in order to present it as the fourth volume in the expanding body of literature which reveals the continuing, continual growth of Goddess-worship among the peoples who treasure the Earth.

道德經, *Tao Te Ching* [*Dào Dé Jīng*]—the "Way of Classic Virtue"—is said to have been written by Lao Tzu ("old boy"), an older contemporary of Confucius, in the 505th Century (6th century BCE). There are no physical remains which can be ascribed to either the body or the life of this Lao Tzu, so it is doubtful that the *Tao Te Ching* was the work of one man, but a compilation of teachings originating in the Taoist school in the kingship of Ch'u.

The *Tao Te Ching* itself barely survived the burning of the books and massacres of the philosophers which the first emperor, Ch'in Shih Huang Ti [Qín Shǐ Huáng Dì], inflicted on the Chinese people. The books of that time were made of thin bamboo strips held together with strings in vertical-columns. Only a few copies of the *Tao* survived the book-burnings, by being buried in the wattle and daub of the mud walls of peasant houses. After the Ch'in Dynasty had been deposed, the books were dug out of the walls. Most of the strings securing the bamboo strips into the correct order, as well as some of the strips themselves, were found to have rotted, and during destruction of the walls to get at the volumes, very many of the remaining strips were separated from the groups to which they belonged. Much effort was put into trying to reassemble the bamboo strips into the correct order, but the *Tao Te Ching* still shows the ravages of the first emperor. I have made no effort to resolve the abrupt changes of topic found in some of the sections (Verse 3 of Poem 36, for example), which were caused by the need to patch the volumes back together: I feel that those are the marks of survival and dedication, and as such are to be cherished.

This text must not be regarded as an attempt at straightforward translation. This should be apparent from its having been given a different name from its primary source. I have had three principle objectives in rewriting the *Tao Te Ching* into the *Ta Men Tao*: to remove the sexist statements which occur in the original, to replace its emphasis on two opposites with the Danaan view of three—of two complements and their interaction—and to fill in some of the poetic holes left by the incomplete restoration done after Ch'in Shi Huang Ti's burning of the books. This restatement of the *Tao Te Ching* in terms of the principles of the Danaan Religion continues forging the bond between the East and West. This process was begun in the *Second Phaedran Letter*, by pairing Danaan Greek and Japanese Shinto terms to show their essential unity, called 大根神道 *Da-Ne-Shin-Tō: the Way of the Deity of the Great Beginning*.

There are some phrases and terms used in the Ta Men Tao which may be unfamiliar to the new reader of my works. Among these are:

The Passage, also referred to as **The Path**: 道 *tao* [*dao*] in Chinese, and *tō* in Japanese. The Passage is the mystic path of the fulfillment of the Universe, the mysterious confluence of all statistical possibilities: the realization of the progress of the **Prime Imperative**: the ever-becoming-ness of the Universe.

The Great Gate: the mystic demarcation of the transit of cycle into cycle, progressing through space and time and their interconnectedness.

The Danaan: Greek = Δαναοί, the Danaans /də.néi.əns/, Homeric Greek adjectival form taken from the early, Doric Greek Δᾶ (Classical Γῆ), who is the Classical, Attic Greek Γαῖα, the Goddess as Mother Earth: Δη-μήτηρ, *Demeter*, literally, *Earth-Mother*. Δᾶ (with duplication *Δᾶδα, then consonantal differentiation, *Δᾶρα) is related to other Mother Goddess names: *Tara* of the Celts, *Tara* (*Taraka*) of Hinduism, and *Tara* [*Devi*] of Tantrism.

The Danaans are those who venerate the Goddess and follow the **Prime Imperative** and its Thirteen Freedoms as ethical basis and guide for their actions in living and loving Life and its Earth. **The Prime Imperative** and **the Thirteen Freedoms** are explained in complete quotations extracted from the *First Phædran Letter* for display on the following pages.

I hope this will make the *Ta Men Tao* more enjoyable
and more enlightening.

PER-ILLAM-ÆTERNAM

ATHENADORUS
Ἀθηνάδωρος

A note on pronunciation:

The romanization system used to represent the Chinese pronunciation of the words referenced above is called the *Wade-Giles* system. Despite its illogic and flaws (*e.g.*, *t'* represents an approximate English *t*-sound (or *t* + *h* sound), while *t* stands for *d*, and the letter *d* isn't used), it was the traditional standard for many years in books about the Chinese language that were written in English; therefore, its representation of many Chinese words has become, unfortunately, more or less standard.

The modern *Pinyin* romanization method is far superior, but does require some training in what sounds certain letters represent. In particular, the Westerner must remember that *c*, *j*, *q*, and *x* represent "soft" (*front* or *aspirated*) versions of *ts*, *zh*, *ch*, and *sh* respectively.

Wade-Giles also uses affixed numbers to denote the tone in which the syllable is spoken, whereas Pinyin uses the far simpler method of four diacritical marks that have a close, graphical correlation to the actual intonation of the voice. [The lack of number (or accent) denotes an unaccented, neutral-tone syllable in both systems.]

With that in mind, here are the Wade-Giles and Pinyin versions of the Chinese words and names referenced above:

traditional	duplicated ("simplified")	Wade-Giles:	Pinyin:
大門道	大门道	Ta[4] Men[2] Tao[4]	Dà Mén Dào
道德經	道德经	Tao[4] Te[2] Ching[1]	Dào Dé Jīng
老子	老子	Lao[3] Tzu	Lǎo Zi
楚[國]	楚[国]	Ch'u[3] [kuo[2]]	Chǔ [guó]
秦始皇帝	秦始皇帝	Ch'in[2] Shih[3] Huang[2] Ti[4]	Qín Shǐ Huáng Dì

THE PRIME IMPERATIVE

3 The **Prime Imperative** is that which all nitrogen-based life must obey: that each living entity will live its life in such a way as to maximize the survival chances of Life itself.

There are three constituent Imperatives which, in balance, *are* the Prime Imperative: that one will live its life so as to maximize the survival chances of one's species (*The Natural Imperative*), one's identity group (*The Social Imperative*), and one's self (*The Personal Imperative*).

The **Prime Imperative** is also called the *Contract of Life* or the *Natural Contract*, for, in receiving the gift of Life, proteins and their more advancing forms abide by this requirement called the ***Prime Imperative***, established by the Goddess at the very birth of the Universe.

There are Thirteen Freedoms which we Danaans hold to be absolutely essential for humans, for them to be able to follow the **Prime Imperative** fully and freely. These thirteen are the social expression of the operative basis of the **Prime Imperative**.

Definition of the *Prime Imperative,* taken from Athenadorus's *First Phædran Letter,* (in *The Athenadoran Library*) which also explains the phrase *nitrogen-based life.*

The Thirteen Freedoms Of The Danaans

1. **FREEDOM OF THOUGHT**: that no government shall attempt to control the minds or mental processes of its people.
2. **FREEDOM OF RELIGION**: that no government shall attempt to establish one religion over another.
3. **FREEDOM OF SPEECH**: that no government shall attempt to stifle the free expression and communication of ideas, or the publication of the truth.
4. **FREEDOM OF ASSEMBLY**: that no government shall limit the right and/or ability of the people peacefully to assemble for just and reasonable purpose.
5. **FREEDOM OF PETITION**: that no government shall limit the ability of the people to address themselves to that government for redress of ills and grievances.
6. **FREEDOM OF POLITICAL ASSOCIATION**: that no government shall attempt to infringe on the right of the people to express alternative viewpoints, publicly or through suffrage, or to form associations for the peaceful furtherance of those viewpoints. Nor shall a government restrict suffrage so as to deny any people their right of alternative expression.
7. **FREEDOM OF PERSONAL IDENTITY**: that no government shall take upon itself the right or power to assign or enforce gender roles, careers or attitudes; to legislate prejudicial discrimination; to legislate moralities; to deprive individuals of ultimate control over their own bodies; or to interfere with the private, non-violent activities of consenting adults.
8. **FREEDOM OF PERSONAL SECURITY**: that no government shall disregard the right of the people to be secure in their persons, effects and property, both real and personal , against unwarranted searches, seizures or any other action of that government without public, free and just due process of the law. Nor shall any government abridge the people's right to own and hold private property.
9. **FREEDOM OF PERSONAL INITIATIVE**: that no government shall deny the people, as individuals in equality, the right to strive for the betterment of their lives or conditions of life, in moving forward to the goal of emotional, physical and financial independence, which is the basis of all hope in human life, and of all progress in human society.
10. **FREEDOM FROM HUNGER**: that a society must be responsible for the prevention of hunger among its people.
11. **FREEDOM FROM DESTITUTION**: that a society must be responsible for the prevention of want for basic necessities among its people.
12. **FREEDOM FROM FEAR**: that a society must exercise its powers and abilities to restrain its government from actions and laws that are detrimental to liberty, to inspire that government to enact legislation which will encourage justice and responsibility, and which will discourage violence among its people.
13. **FREEDOM FROM IGNORANCE**: that a society must exert itself fully in striving to educate its people; and must work to diminish the effects and influence of those who espouse ignorance.

Exposition of the *Thirteen Freedoms of the Danaans*, from Athenadorus's *First Phædra Letter*.

1

1. The spirit that has but one name is not the Eternal Spirit.
   The name that can be named is not the Eternal Name.
2. The Nameless is the beginning of the Universe.
   The All-name is the Mother of the heavens and the Earth.
   The Naming is the fulfillment of all destiny.
3. Ever desireless, one feels Her Mystery.
   Ever desiring, one sees Her Clarity.
   Ever desired, one fulfills the Unity.
4. These three flow from the Origin,
   different only in form.
5. The face in darkness:
   Shadow-mother of shadow,
   Gate of all Mystery.

2

1. All can recognize beauty because they know the Passage.
2. Beauty and non-beauty ebb and flow through the Great Gate:
the golden portal of distinguishability,
the sweet grape-cluster of Middle Action—
where the beautiful and non-beautiful mix and create
the soul of distinguishing,
the mind of realization.
3. Who has only slavery knows nothing of freedom:
Who sees only freedom knows nothing of slavery.
4. It is upon knowledge of both, the co-mingling of waters,
that stands the Great Hall of the Liberation.
5. Who sees not freedom cannot long to be free.
Who have not rejected slavery
cannot cherish the freedom they possess.
6. The Hall of the People is only so strong
as the will of the people themselves.
7. We know good as good
because we know the Middle Passage.
8. We have seen the Gate and fathomed its secret:
it unites the fields as it divides them.
9. Having and not-having are co-equal.
Difficult and easy are the same.
Long and short are children of the One.
High and low are of the same mountain.
Voice and noise are singers of one song.
Front and back live in the Unity of the One.
10. Thus We teach and do not teach
and it is the same.
11. All things rise and fall, never ceasing:
never ceasing the Passage, joining between.
12. Creating, but not claiming.
Accomplishing, but never demanding reward.
13. Changes are made,
and are changed in the making:
in its tranquility it is eternal.

3

1. Not praising the talented prevents quarreling.
   Not amassing treasures prevents stealing.
   Ignoring desirable things prevents confusion in the mind.
2. Yet, why should fear of robbery prohibit collecting?
   Or fear of confusion prohibit seeking desirable things?
3. The wise will lead by praising the Passage:
   for it is in understanding the extremes-inherent
   that middle peace is brought to light.
4. We lead therefore by knowing hearts,
   channeling ambitions,
   strengthening resolve.
5. If the people lack knowledge and the desire for it,
   intellectuals cannot interfere:
   the people will be moved by fear.
6. Act in non-action
   and all will know peace.

4

1. The Passage is a full, flowing spring:
   use will never drain it.
2. Boundless Source of the Universe!
   Reveal our gentleness!
   Simplify our outlook!
   Increase our subtlety!
   Make us One with your transcendent Universe!
3. Deeply hidden companion,
   ever within us,
   I know not whence you come:
   You are the first Mother of the people!

5

1. The Universe is remorseless:
   the delusions of men are nothingness.
2. The Danaans are remorseless:
   the lies of men are shown to be nothingness.
3. The Earth and the heavens are like a cloud,
   changing in form, but not in self.
4. The more it moves, the more it yields.
5. Learn constancy from the silence:
   stand strong with the Passage.

6

1. The Passage Spirit is immortal:
   She is Woman, Primal Mystery,
   Gateway foundation of the Universe.
2. The Passage is a veil of mist, ephemeral shimmering:
   Path of Cycle into Cycle.
3. Follow Her: She will never fail.

7

1. The Universe lasts forever.
2. How does the Universe last forever?
   Because it knows Birth, yet was not born,
   has felt Death, yet cannot die.
   Thus it is ever alive.
3. We stand at the rear,
   thus we take the lead.
4. We are at one with the past,
   therefore first into the future.
5. We are detached,
   thus at one with all:
   reaching beyond self,
   through the sharing,
   out toward Unity.
6. In the voyage that leads to Unity,
   discover fulfillment.

8

1. The Passage is like water:
   it gives life to the Universe and does not fuss.
2. It flows through all things,
   remembered, not unforgotten.
   And thus is like the Imperative Prime.
3. In living, cherish the Earth.
   In meditation, dive deep into the mind.
   In friendship, be gentle and mindful of the bond.
   In speaking, worship truth.
   In judgment, justice.
   In leading, humility.
   In commerce, competence.

9

1. Better not to fill than to spill.
   The oversharpened blade blunts first.
   Treasures of gold are soonest filched.
2. Claim the undue and disaster follows.
3. Go to sleep when day is done:
   the Moon will hold the sky till morning.

10

1. Mind, body and soul in your Unity,
   can you embrace the One and remain whole?
2. Listening and recognizing ignorance,
   can you return to your childhood?
3. Scrubbing and rinsing away the ancient hatred,
   can you be without stain?
4. Loving all the people and leading the nation,
   can you do so without arrogance?
5. Opening and closing the windows of the Universe,
   can you explain the Unity of the Goddess?
6. Understanding and being receptive to all things,
   can you act in tranquility?
7. To give birth, guidance and nourishment,
   to hold without struggling to possess,
   to labor without demanding recognition,
   to lead without lessening the people's freedom.
   This is the Prime Imperative: mystical virtue.

11

1. All the spokes share the wheel-hub:
   it is the hole that gives it usefulness.
2. Form clay into a bowl:
   it is the volume-possibility within
   that creates utility.
3. Cut doors and windows in the walls that form a room:
   the walls give it substance,
   the holes, purpose.
   And profit lies in the difference between the two.

12

1. The infinite colors can blind,
   the infinite tones can deafen,
   the infinite flavors can dull the appetite.
2. Ever-racing and hunting destroy tranquility.
   Ever-grasping for precious things leads one from the Path.
3. Thus we eat without gorging,
   read but do not tire the mind,
   show affection when affection is due.
4. Only from the Middle are all boundaries in view.

13

1. Acknowledge failure without despair;
   look on misfortune as opportunity in human life:
   for the surmounting of calamity
   is the triumph of humanity,
   and turning to face our problems—
   the very soul of victory.
2. Disease is as much a part of life
   as ease is integral to existence.
3. As ease is a challenge to self-discipline,
   disease is an opportunity to strengthen devotion.
4. Who loves the people more than
   ruling the people
   can be trusted with the people.
5. Who loves the Earth more than
   dominion over the Earth
   can be trusted with the life of the Earth.

14

1. The shape invisible, transcending form.
   The quiet inaudible, transcending silence.
   The grasp intangible, transcending touch.
   These are beyond description,
   yet are described in the One.
2. Its summit is not blinding,
   its base is not obscure.
3. Interconnected streams intertwined
   distinct in undecipherability,
   becoming again that which is becoming.
4. The formless form,
   the shapeless shape,
   the unseeable image.
5. The fathoming of shadows,
   pottery-molding of mists.
6. Draw near it, you see no beginning.
   Draw away from it, you see no end.
7. Preserve the quiet Stream from the Past:
   the ability to be One with the Beginning
   is the source of Unity with the Passage.

15

1. The ancient ones, well-versed in the Passage
   were subtle observers,
   mysteriously cognizant,
   profoundly powerful.
2. Because we cannot fully fathom their knowledge,
   we can only describe its workings:
   halting, like those crossing a frozen stream,
   cautious, as if realizing the nearness of danger,
   formal, like a courteous guest,
   yielding, like snow in the sun,
   resolute, like the uncarved block,
   open, like a mountain valley,
   veiled, like a muddy stream.
3. Who can be enfogged and yet quietly await the clearing?
   Who can be tranquil until moving with the defense?
4. Who knows the Passage seeks neither starvation
   nor to be stuffed full.
5. It is because they knew the Passage
   that the ancient ones could be worn out,
   then completely made new.

16

1. We commit ourselves to attain peace:
   we grasp firmly the rest within quietude.
2. The numberless creatures arise, soaring together:
   we are One with their return.
3. Numberless, each returns
   to its separate, common origin,
   the Origin which is the Self.
4. Returning to the Origin produces tranquility.
5. The Passage of the Return is constant,
   constantly evolving:
   knowledge of the Constant is the Mother of Wisdom.
6. Wisdom is self-identity within the Goddess.
   Willful ignorance is disastrous folly.
7. Who works from knowledge of the Constant
   will be led into equanimity,
   from equanimity to compassion,
   from compassion to love of Nature,
   from love of Nature to the Way of the Prime Imperative.
8. And the Way of the Prime Imperative
   leads to Oneness with the Goddess,
   which is Peace Eternal:
   for the Passage will never fail.

17

1. The best ruler is the least ruling:
   the most forgotten, the least intruding.
   The next is one known and loved.
   The next is one feared.
   The next is one revolted against.
2. When new laws are made,
   more of the old laws will be broken.
3. The best leader is hesitant to speak,
   guarding words carefully in all actions:
   thus the people will think the accomplishments
   were all their own
   and that thought will be true.

18

1. When justice and compassion are everywhere present,
   the Passage may be forgotten.
2. When cleverness and selective ignorance are nurtured,
   the great paranoid hypocrisy flourishes.
3. When some family members squabble,
   others will become caring.
4. When the nation is threatened,
   loyal officials will arise.

19

1. Renounce learning,
   and ignorance will no longer trouble you.
2. Renounce wisdom and sagacity,
   and everyone will seem a hundred times more wise.
3. Renounce compassion and benevolence,
   and everyone will seem to be pious and caring again.
4. Renounce ingenuity and profit,
   and bandits and thieves will have no one to rob.
5. These actions deal with outward form only:
   this is not, in itself, enough.
6. Be unaffected, unadorned,
   quiet in warm simplicity,
   fully living the truth of Nature:
   strong like the uncarved block,
   throwing off selfishness by loving the Path:
   moderating ambition and desire.

20

1. How great is the gap between yes and no?
   How wide is the gulf between good and evil?
2. Should we fear the nightmares of others? Never!
3. Others seem happy, sharing common festivals,
   going to the park in Spring, climbing the terraces.
4. I alone show no movement, reveal no emotion,
   like an infant before it awakens to smiles.
5. Without residence, I drift alone.
6. So many have far more than they need—
   I alone seem to have nothing.
7. I seem a fool: simplicity seems confused.
8. Others appear to be incisive and clever—
   but I, alone, seem plodding and dull:
   calm yet restless like the waves of the Sea,
   driven like the ceaseless wind.
10. The masses think they have purpose:
    they think that I, alone, am aimless,
    deserted, despairing.
11. But I am different from all others:
    I know the nourishment of the Mother of the Universe.

21

1. In every way, greatest virtue is
   to follow the Passage and only the Passage.
2. The Path is flitting shadow, untouchable.
   Untouchable shadow, yet cradling an image.
3. Shadowy untouchable, yet filled with substance.
   Dim and dark, yet nurturing the Fundament.
4. The Fundament is very Truth,
   within which lies Faith,
   answering, testable.
5. Throughout all ages She has never been forgotten:
   She is the Guide for leading the people.
6. How do I know this?
   From the Passage.

22

1. Yielding to overcome,
   bending to straighten,
   hollowing to fill,
   being worn to renew,
   having little to receive benefit:
   having too much perplexes.
2. Thus We embrace the Unity
   and are an example to the people.
3. Avoiding empty display,
   we are conspicuous to all.
4. Not being self-righteous,
   we are illustrious.
5. Not bragging,
   we attain recognition.
6. Not boasting,
   we do not stumble.
7. Because we are not contentious,
   we are unified in compassion.
8. We conquer pride to master ourselves.
9. Thus the ancients said,
   "Yield if you would overcome."
10. Know yourself:
    and your self will be completely yours.

23

1. To talk but sparingly is natural.
2. The wind cannot gust all week,
   nor can a rainstorm thunder all month.
3. What is the source of these things?
   The Universe.
4. If even the Universe does not create things eternal,
   how then can humanity?
5. Therefore, we become One with the Goddess.
6. Who walks the Passage is One with the Passage:
   Who is virtuous is one with Virtue.
7. Who is part of the Universe is the Universe.
8. If you do not trust others,
   others will not trust you.

24

1. The one on tiptoe is not steady.
   Who runs cannot measure the stride.
   The arrogant is not circumspect.
   The pompous is not respected.
   The boaster has no value:
   the braggart will not endure.
2. To those at One with the Passage,
   these are impediments, useless baggage.
3. These things are detestable bringers of sorrow.
   We do not abide them.

25

1. It was mysteriously shaped,
   born before the Universe.
2. Silent in the void,
   existence singular and unchanging,
   presence eternal and ever-changing,
   it is capable of giving birth to all universes.
3. We know not what it calls itself.
   So we call it the Passage,
   and create the term great.
4. Great, it recedes into the distance.
   Recedent, it seems far away.
   Seeming far away, it is also returning.
5. Thus the Passage is great,
   the Universe is great,
   the Earth is great,
   and the people are great.
6. These are the great ones of the Kosmos
   and the people are among them.
7. Humanity moves with the Earth,
   the Earth moves with the Universe,
   the Universe moves with the Passage,
   for the Passage is All-Truth.

26

1. Heaviness is the source of lightness.
   Tranquility is the master of restlessness.
2. Thus the wayfarer on the road
   does not forget to pack for the journey.
3. Though beauty awaits to draw one's eyes away,
   the wayfarer remains unperturbed.
4. Why should the master of 10,000 wisdoms
   act lightly toward that mastery in the eyes of the masses?
5. If light, the root will be lost.
   Lightness will let the base crumble.
6. Restlessness will destroy self-control.

27

1. The good hiker leaves no trace.
   The good speaker leaves no confusion.
   The good counter needs no tally.
2. The best closer needs use no locks,
   yet once closed, it cannot be opened.
3. The best binder knots no cords,
   yet once bound, it cannot be loosed.
4. Thus we have compassion for all people
   and abandon none.
5. We conserve all living things
   and abandon none.
6. This is called following the Passage.
7. The pious teaches the impious.
   The impious is the raw material of the teacher.
8. To disparage the teacher,
   to despise the material,
   each is the source of confusion.
9. These are the foundation of ignorance.

28

1. Know the strength,
   but cherish the tenderness.
2. Be the heart of the Universe.
3. As the heart of the Universe,
   unflagging Truth will be ever with you,
   you who are like little children once more.
4. Know the bright,
   but keep the role of the shadow.
5. Be the ideal of the people.
6. As the ideal of the people,
   constant and steadfast,
   you reunite with the Infinite.
7. Know honor,
   but understand humility and disgrace.
8. Be the fertile valley of the Universe.
9. As the fertile valley of the Universe,
   constancy and incisiveness suffice
   to return to the uncarved block.
10. When the block is worked,
    it splits into many vessels.
11. We use these and become master of Self,
    of the uncarved, carved block:
    the greatest cut does not sever.

29

1. Who would seize the Universe and make it over
is a restless fool.
2. The Universe is sacred:
do nothing that might mar it.
3. Who would alter it
will be ruined in the trying.
4. Who would grasp it
will lose it.
5. Some lead, some follow,
some stay behind.
6. Some breathe gently, some breathe fiercely,
some breathe without design.
7. Some are strong, some are weak,
some have never tested themselves.
8. Sometimes one destroys, sometimes one is destroyed,
sometimes one transcends the extremes.
9. We avoid emphasizing the extremes,
ostentation and arrogance.

30

1. The wise leader does not rattle sabres
to frighten people:
the use of arms always rebounds.
2. Tares and thistles are the legacy of armies encamped.
Hunger is the harvest sown, tended and reaped by war.
3. The best army is disbanded when marching is through.
4. Do only what must be done,
then let the people rest.
5. Get things done:
but do not be pompous.
6. Get things done:
but do not boast.
7. Get things done:
but do not be self-righteous.
8. Get things done:
but not in foolish haste.
9. Get things done:
but never through terror.
10. The strong hurting the weak, young and old,
is going against the Passage.
11. Those not with the Passage
will be overcome by the Passage.

31

1. Powerful weapons are instruments of terror:
   we do not trust in them.
2. We give honor to the olive branch in the left hand
   over the rifle in the right.
3. Weapons are the tools of terror:
   they are unnatural implements.
4. When compelled to use them, it is only
   because we have no other choice.
5. There is no glory in conquerors' triumphs,
   for they celebrate slaughter.
6. Who exults in battle-gore is not sane.
7. But our Danaan delight
   is Freedom within Peace:
   of farming the great land, broad and green,
   of arts and commerce that make lives and bellies full,
   of bright-eyed children's laughter.
8. When people are killed,
   we weep for them in sorrow.
9. When victorious in war,
   we mourn for those lost by all.

32

1. The Passage is forever limitless.
2. Though at times perceived as small,
   it cannot be confined.
3. If the people were able to grasp its meaning,
   the Universe would be seen to obey it and no other.
4. Heaven and Earth would be known as One
   and the sweet rain of enlightenment would fall.
5. Justice would walk among the people:
   natural compassion and respect prevail,
   without interfering decree.
6. Once the uncarved block is cut,
   the parts need names.
7. Once names are realized,
   one must realize when to rest.
8. Knowing when to rest
   is liberation from distress.
9. The Passage is to the Universe
   as the Ocean is to the rivers:
   end, substance and source.

33

1. To understand others is discernment:
   to know oneself is wisdom.
2. To subdue others is force:
   to conquer oneself is strength paramount.
3. Who has contentment has wealth.
   Who perseveres has tenacity.
4. Who maintains resolve will endure.
   Who lives at peace will have a full life.

34

1. The Passage flows broad,
   to the left, to the right and ahead.
2. All Life depends on it,
   yet it demands nothing in return.
3. It brings all tasks to completion,
   yet begs no reward.
4. It nourishes the multitude of creatures,
   yet binds no lien.
5. Ever selfless in action,
   one could call it minute.
6. Yet in not wanting to be master of the multitude dependent,
   it is infinite indeed.
7. It is not self-righteous or grasping,
   and in that it is truly great.

35

1. Hold to the Passage and all peoples will come to you:
   for in you they will find peace and compassion.
2. Casual travelers may be lured by loud music and food,
   but the Passage does not entice the multitude
   with temporary aromas and fleeting flavors.
3. The Passage cannot be directly observed in its entirety.
   The Passage cannot be quickly heard of in its infinity.
   Nor can use exhaust it.

36

1. What shrinks must first be large.
   What weakens must first be strong.
   What is thrown off must first be taken up.
   What is received must first be given.
2. This is subtle understanding:
   the yielding and weak can surpass the hard and strong.
3. Fish can survive only surrounded by water:
   the nation's defense will be strong
   only when never put on display.

37

1. The Passage takes no action,
   yet nothing is left undone.
2. If leaders understood this
   all things would occur without struggle.
3. If the leaders still would use force,
   they will be tamed by the uncarved block.
4. The Passage is freedom from obsession.
5. Without obsession, one attains peace of mind
   and all settles in warm tranquility.

38

1. The truly just are just
   because they nurture justice.
2. The foolish try to be just
   because they wish to appear just.
3. The truly benevolent take no action
   yet nothing is left undone.
4. The foolish take many actions
   yet much is left undone.
5. The truly compassionate take action
   only from the loftiest motive.
6. The foolish take action
   only from selfishness.
7. The patriarchal acts officiously,
   and when disproved, retrenches
   and tries to enforce insanity with violence.
8. When the Passage is forgotten,
   compassion remains.
9. When compassion is forgotten,
   kindness remains.
10. When kindness is forgotten,
    reason remains.
11. When reason is forgotten,
    ritual superstition remains.
12. Ritual superstition is the chaff
    of the harvests of the human mind:
    the seed of ignorance.
13. Foreknowledge is only a flower beside the Path:
    to feature it is folly.
14. We assert the substance more than the surface:
    the pulp of the fruit more than the perfume of the flower.
15. Therefore we cherish truth
    and reject falsehood.

39

1. All things have their beginning
   in the most ancient One.
2. The heavens are open and clear
   through the One.
3. The Earth is perfect and serene
   through the One.
4. The divine ones are steadfast and strong
   through the One.
5. This vale is wide and fertile
   through the One.
6. The multitude of creatures is vibrant and alive
   through the One.
7. The people become leaders of the nations
   through the One:
   their qualities are all drawn
   from the Qualities of the One.
8. Without the One, nothing that exists could exist.
9. That which has superiority must have humility,
   as well as that in-between.
10. That which is high must also be low
    as well as that in-between.
11. Some describe themselves
    alone, despised, rejected:
    they emphasize the negative-extreme,
    forgetting the width of the Path.
12. Too much of that desired destroys desire.
13. Therefore, do not force the future:
    all things in their own good time.

40

1. The Passage goes forward by returning.
   Yielding to Truth is the way the Passage moves.
2. The Universe was born from that which is.
   And that which is was born by that
   which always has been.

41

1. The wise student realizes the Prime Imperative
   and travels the Passage diligently.
2. The average student hears about the Prime Imperative
   and occasionally thinks about the Passage.
3. The foolish student hears of the Prime Imperative
   and laughs aloud.
4. If the ignorant did not laugh at it,
   the Passage would not be true.
5. Thus it is written that
   the brightest seems dim,
   the advancing seems to retreat,
   the smoothest seems pitted,
   the highest seems base,
   the purest seems sullied,
   the most abundant seems insufficient,
   the most robust seems weary,
   the most unaffected seems pompous.
6. The perfect square has no corners.
   The greatest work takes longest to complete.
   The greatest melody is rarely heard.
   The greatest existence has no boundaries.
7. The Passage seems hidden and indescribable.
   But only the Passage brings about,
   nourishes
   and carries to completion.

42

1. The Passage begot the One.
   The One begot the Three.
   The Three begot the Nine.
   The All begot the Infinite.
2. The multitude carries yin and embraces yang
   and exists through the Third: the Unity of the One.
3. All people would hate to be alone, despised, rejected,
   yet this is how some try to grasp the devotion of the world.
4. One gains in detracting,
   and becomes detracted in gaining.
5. As others have said, so say I:
   the violent shall meet death in violence.
6. This is the foundation of Her temple.

43

1. The most yielding can conquer
   the most obdurate in the Universe:
   the intangible penetrating the seemingly impermeable.
2. This is the blessing of non-contention.
3. The tutor who is mute,
   the unstruggling laborer.

44

1. Your reputation or your Self—
   which is more important to you?
2. Your Self or your possessions—
   which is more valuable to you?
3. Gain or loss—
   which is more troublesome?
4. The miser will suffer most loss:
   the pecunious will be much bereft.
5. Learn contentment
   and you will never be dissatisfied.
6. Learn when to rest
   and you will not encounter trouble:
   you will persevere.

45

1. The perfect seems flawed,
   but it does not wear with use.
2. The filled seems empty,
   yet it does not drain with drinking.
3. The linear seems curved.
   The wise seems foolish.
   The eloquent seems to stutter.
4. Movement conquers coolness:
   calmness conquers warmth.
5. Calm and clear of vision,
   one can lead the people.

46

1. When the Path is cherished,
   draft-horses work in the fields.
2. When the Path is ignored,
   war-horses trample the crops.
3. There is nothing more destructive than unbridled desire.
   Nothing more calamitous than being discontent.
   No greater affliction than jealous greed.
4. Who knows when to rest
   will always find tranquility.

47

1. Without opening your eyes,
   you can possess the Universe.
2. Without looking out the window,
   you can hold the Path of the Universe.
3. The farther one goes into it,
   the less one knows.
4. Thus we share
   without having to be present,
   understand without struggle,
   achieve without contention.

48

1. In the pursuit of knowledge,
   learn one thing more every day.
2. In following the Passage,
   let go of one thing more every day.
3. One does less and less until nothingness is achieved:
   when nothing at all is done,
   nothing will be left undone.
4. The people are led by not interfering:
   they will not be led by meddling.

49

1. The Danaan is not one mind, alone:
   but reaches out, to share the hopes of the people.
2. I see as good those whose actions are good.
   I also see as good those whose actions are not good.
   Thus we all increase in benevolence.
3. I trust in those who are faithful.
   I also trust in those who are not faithful.
   Thus we all increase in fidelity.
4. Our message seems intricate,
   complicated, confusing.
5. Its simplicity is not apparent to the people
   because, like children, they are drawn away
   by flashing lights and the pressure of the crowd.

50

1. In choosing between enjoying life and glorifying death,
   one of the three now clings to life,
   one of the three now charges toward death,
   and one of the three travels the Passage—
   from transition, through life, to transition.
2. Why is this so?
3. Because the third one has transcended
   the base level of short-sightedness.
4. We who know the Passage walk about unafraid:
   unafraid of the rhinoceros or tiger,
   unafraid of battle wounds.
5. For we cannot be gored without our knowledge,
   we cannot be scratched without our approval:
   no weapons will pierce us unless we allow it.
6. Why is this so?
7. Because we are One with the Passage.

51

1. In the Passage is all Life.
2. Raised up by energy,
   given form by matter,
   shaped by transformation.
3. Thus all creatures abide in the Prime Imperative
   and honor the Passage:
   not because it has been forced on them
   by laws or words,
   but because the Passage is within the creatures
   and the creatures are One with the Passage.
4. The Prime Imperative creates all living things:
   gives them form and individuality,
   nurses them, guides them, fosters them,
   changes them, develops them, nourishes them.
5. Creating without claiming possession.
   Doing without demanding recompense.
   Leading without interfering.
6. These live in the Primal Mystery.

52

1. The birth of the Universe is the Mother of all that exists.
2. When you understand the Mother,
   you will understand Her Children.
3. When you know the Children and are One with the Mother,
   you will find liberation from the fear of death.
4. Build a quiet intelligence,
   be protective of your senses,
   and your life will not be meaningless.
5. Overwhelm your senses,
   grow in non-understanding,
   and you will have an empty life.
6. Who sees the small is perceptive.
   Who yields to conquer is strong.
7. Surrounded by light,
   we see the inner glow.
8. Warm within the Passage,
   we follow the constant One.

53

1. If I had only the least bit of common sense,
   I would still walk only along the great, wide Passage,
   and my only concern would be not to stray from it.
2. The great Passage is easily kept to,
   yet people call the broad boulevard of ignorance
   straight and narrow.
3. Where the government is aloof,
   weeds rule the fields
   and the granaries stand empty.
4. Still there are those who are showily dressed,
   wearing gaudy appointments,
   gorged on food and drink:
   hoarding possessions.
5. They are the robber-chieftains of the people.
6. This is far from the Path of the Prime Imperative.

54

1. That deeply rooted cannot be pulled up.
   That tightly held cannot slip away.
2. Therefore the honor bestowed
   will be cherished through all generations.
3. Cultivate the Passage in your life,
   and it will be wonderfully alive.
4. Cultivate the Passage in your family,
   and it will be strengthened.
5. Cultivate the Passage in your community,
   and it will prosper.
6. Cultivate the Passage in your nation,
   and it will be honored.
7. Cultivate the Passage in your everything,
   and everything will be recognized in the Unity.
8. Therefore recognize the individual in the individual.
   Recognize the family in the family.
   Recognize the nation in the nation.
   Recognize the everything in the Everything.
9. How do I know the Universe is this way?
   Through the Prime Imperative
   and the fulfillment of the Passage.

55

1. One living the Passage is like the newborn babe:
   stinging things are kept far away from it–
   wild animals are not permitted to pounce upon it–
   soaring birds are not allowed to prey on it.
2. Its bones are weak,
   its muscles are weak,
   but its grip is strong.
3. It has not enjoyed sexual union,
   yet it knows excitement:
   its individuality has been established.
4. It can cry all day without becoming hoarse:
   because it is in harmony with its existence.
5. To know harmony is to achieve the Constant.
   To know constancy is to achieve the Unity.
6. To overemphasize the self is foolishness.
   The foolish mind self-centered is the root of violence.
7. The strong hurting the weak, young and old,
   is going against the Passage.
8. Those not with the Passage
   will be overcome by the Passage.

56

1. Who knows rations words.
   Who blithers has no thoughts.
2. Sit quietly,
   restraining sensations.
3. Find your gentleness,
   simplify your outlook,
   become more subtle.
4. Be One with the transcendent Universe.
   This is the Mystery of the Prime Imperative.
5. Unapproachable and unescapable.
   Unimprovable and undamageable.
   Un-ennoblable and uncursable.
6. Its Unity is the Summit.

57

1. Govern the people with justice.
   Wage war with stealth.
2. The people will be won by protecting their rights.
3. How do I know this? From this:
4. The more laws there are,
   the poorer the people become.
5. The more deadly the weapons are,
   the more fear stalks the land.
6. The more deceitful the people must be,
   the more new lies abound.
7. The more rules and regulations are imposed,
   the more criminals there are.
8. Thus the wise One says,
9. I take no action
   and the people return to the Passage.
10. I am tranquil
    and the people rekindle Justice.
11. I do not interfere
    and the people attain Prosperity.
12. I desire nothing but that the people rediscover Simplicity,
    Forthrightness and Peace.

58

1. When the government acts seldom,
   the people are forthright.
2. When the government acts minutely,
   the people are deceitful.
3. Fortune flowers from misfortune.
   Beneath happiness lies the knowledge of sadness.
4. Who can know how things will be?
5. Truthfulness does not abide forever of itself:
   the truthful can become a liar,
   and fortune become disaster.
6. For many centuries now,
   the children have cherished the disaster of ignorance.
7. We, however,
   perpetuate our fortunate understanding.
8. We are incisive, but do not cut.
   We are piercing, but do not stab.
9. We grow in number, but protect the liberty of all.
   We shine brightly, but do not blind.

59

1. In leading the people of Earth,
   there is no gift that surpasses self-control.
2. Using self-control from the beginning,
   one follows the Passage.
3. Following the Passage from the beginning,
   one lives the Prime Imperative.
4. When one lives the Prime Imperative,
   there is nothing that cannot be overcome.
5. Able to overcome all things,
   tranquility will ensue.
6. Bestower of tranquility,
   one can lead the people.
7. The principles of good government are ever true,
   ever the same.
8. Bestowing tranquility to the people
   is the great foundation of their affection.
9. The Passage is eternally visible in their affection.

60

1. Leading the people is like handling a cooked fish.
2. Stand before the people within the Passage
   and the impious will lose all power.
3. It is not that they lose their power,
   but that they cannot harm the people.
4. It is not only the impious
   who will not harm the people:
   the wise One as well will not harm the people.
5. The Three will find the benevolence within each other
   and all will be gladdened.

61

1. A great people is like a broad river valley:
   collecting the separate streams of existence
   into the River of the Unity of Existence.
2. One surpasses another by yielding.
3. Conquering, one may take a lower position.
4. By being pliant, a larger nation can annex the smaller.
   The smaller, by yielding, can absorb the larger.
5. Who conquers, yields.
6. The large country would better use its resources.
   The small country would provide more for its people.
7. In the balance, each may succeed in its goals.
8. It is a great deed when a larger nation graciously yields.

62

1. The Passage is the Mother of all things.
   It is the strength of the pious,
   the safe haven of the impious.
2. Flattering words may obtain high rank.
   Flattering deeds may purchase promotion.
3. Even so, do not abandon the impious.
4. On the day the Archelaa is raised up
   and the councils are installed,
   gifts of fine jade and prancing chargers
   are not needed.
5. The tranquil gift of the Passage
   is the best that can be given.
6. Why has the Passage been loved for so long?
   There is no reason other than that
   it gives you what you seek,
   and does not damn you if you forget.
7. It is the great treasure of the people.

63

1. Act in non-action.
   Accomplish without interfering.
2. Savor that without taste.
   Magnify the small.
   Multiply the few.
   Return benevolence for injury.
3. Do the difficult while still simple:
   build the great up from the small.
4. Complex things arise from the simple.
   The large arises from the small.
5. We strive to understand the simple
   and the small:
   thus become great,
   understanding the complex.
6. Making light promises damages trust.
   Taking all lightly brings on complications.
7. We confront the complicated as complicated,
   still striving to grasp its simple roots:
   and thereby conquer all difficulties.

64

1. Maintain peace while still at peace.
   Deal with trouble before it arises.
2. Still new and brittle is easily broken.
   Still young and small is easily dispersed.
3. Deal with it before it happens:
   keeping in order will prevent disorder.
4. The tree thicker than one's embrace
   arose from tender shoot.
5. The palace nine stories high
   was once a pile of dirt.
6. A journey of a thousand miles
   begins beneath one's own feet.
7. Who contends is defeated.
   Who clutches it will lose it.
8. We are not contentious,
   thus never conquered.
9. We are not clutching,
   thus nothing ever slips away from us.
10. Failure most often rides the verge of success.
11. Nurse the end as well as the beginning,
    then failure will never learn your name.
12. We dare not to be ruled by desire:
    not to care about scarce bric-a-brac,
    not to be afraid of learning new ideas,
    of daring to revive the precious of the past.
13. We dare to help the multitude
    return to Nature
    and cease to contend.

65

1. Some ancients claimed to have knowledge of the Path.
2. They used this claim not to enlighten,
   but to deceive.
3. To lead the people is a great challenge:
   they are not fools.
4. To govern by deception
   is to endanger the nation.
5. To govern without guile
   is to bless the people.
6. These two are the extremes.
7. To recognize the extremes of the Continuum
   is the beginning of mysterious union with the Passage.
8. The Passage is profound,
   ever-extensive, ever-co-extensive.
9. Going, existing and returning with all things,
   creating the great Unity.

66

1. The Ocean receives all waters
   because it is in the lower position.
   Thus it is the master of the rivers.
2. If you would lead the people,
   you must preside with humility.
3. If you would be a good leader,
   be the best follower.
4. With a Danaan leading,
   the people will not know oppression.
5. With a Danaan leading,
   the people's dreams will not find hindrance.
6. Thus the people will give support enthusiastically
   and will not be wearied by it.
7. It is because we are not contentious
   that we are strong in our Unity.

67

1. Some say my teaching
   is vast and incomparable.
2. It is vast because of my subject:
   there is nothing that can be compared with it.
3. If it were not without equal,
   we would long ago have disappeared.
4. There are three treasures I nurture and cherish.
   The first is compassion.
   The second is thrift.
   The third is daring to have humility.
5. Compassion engenders courage.
   Thrift bestows generosity.
   Humility confers pre-eminence among the people.
6. To abandon compassion for bravado,
   to abandon thrift for waste,
   to abandon humility for fame,
   all will surely lead to death.
7. Compassion gives triumph in battle,
   impregnable defense,
   and tranquility in all occasions.
8. It is the Goddess nourishing the people.

68

1. The best soldier is not bloodthirsty.
   The best fighter is not angry.
   The best competitor is not vengeful.
   The best employer does not forget humility.
2. This is the strength of non-contention:
   the ability to love the people.
3. It is the ultimate sublimity of the Path.

69

1. The strategists often say,
   I dare not plan as the host,
   but must play the part of the invader.
2. I dare not advance
   without knowing retreat as well.
3. This is marching without raising the dust:
   rolling up sleeves with no shirt,
   defeating the invisible foe,
   being armed without bearing arms.
4. There is no disaster greater
   than underestimating the resources of the enemy:
   doing so has nearly cost us our treasure,
   and has cost us many treasured.
5. When two peoples take up arms against each other,
   it is the aggrieved one that will prevail.

70

1. My words are clear,
   my precepts easily applied.
2. Yet no one understands them
   or puts them to practice.
3. My words have prehistoric ancestors,
   my actions have a sovereign's discipline.
4. People do not know me:
   they do not dare try to understand.
5. Those who adopt my words are few.
   Those who deride my words are honored.
6. Despite all this, I,
   though wearing homespun and rags,
   conceal the priceless treasure of the Heart.

71

1. To measure one's own ignorance gives strength:
   to disregard one's own ignorance makes weak.
2. Being on guard, one can prevent trouble.
3. We meet no trouble that cannot be tamed.
   For we are ever watchful.

72

1. When the people have lost appreciation
   of the awesomeness of Nature,
   disaster will descend upon them.
2. Do not invade the privacy of the home.
   Do not distress the people's well-being.
3. If you do not overburden them,
   they will not weary.
4. Thus we know ourselves,
   but are not out on display.
5. We have self-respect,
   but are not presumptuous.
6. We have let go of this
   and chosen that.

73

1. The presumptuous brave carries early death.
   The humble brave will protect long life.
2. In any moment, death comes to some
   and not to others.
3. The course of Nature is the course of Nature.
   Why ask That-beyond-Justice for justification?
   Even We must sometimes strive with this.
4. The Passage seeks no struggle,
   yet always overcomes.
5. It does not speak,
   yet answers all questions.
6. It issues no command,
   yet is always obeyed.
7. It seems haphazard,
   yet is itself Perfect Law.
8. The fabric of the Universe is finitely infinite:
   though the weave does not seem tight,
   nothing ever slips through.

74

1. If the people do not fear death,
   why try to frighten them with the threat of execution?
2. If the people feared death,
   and if committing a crime were grounds for execution,
   who would dare?
3. There is an official executioner
   whose place cannot be usurped.
4. If one would try, it would be like
   a novice attempting to cut wood
   as if a master carpenter:
   few would escape without grief.

75

1. The people are starving.
2. Because the government eats the money in taxes,
   the people are starving.
3. The people are rebellious.
4. Because the government interferes in their lives,
   the people are rebellious.
5. The people are indifferent toward death.
6. Because the government uses them as sacrifices,
   the people are indifferent toward death.
7. In the cold shadow of the ignorants' boasts,
   they know better than to cling to life too strongly.

76

1. Humans are pliant, weak when alive,
   hard and stiff when dead.
2. Plants are pliable, fragile when alive,
   hard and stiff when dead.
3. The hard, unyielding is the disciple of death.
   The supple, yielding is the associate of Life.
4. The unadaptive weapon will not help to win.
   The straight, unbending tree will know the axe.
5. The stiff, unyielding will be overturned.
   The supple, yielding will be victorious.

77

1. The Path is like the testing of a bow:
   it lowers the lofty,
   it exalts the low,
   it decreases the oppressive,
   it increases the compassionate,
   it exchanges excess and destroys deficit.
2. The Man would do it differently:
   he takes from the needy
   to give to the wealthy.
3. Who are those who will take their own wealth
   and share it with the people?
   Only those who know the Passage.
4. Thus we assist without asking recompense,
   and do the work without demanding acclaim.
5. This is because our first love
   is the liberty within equality.

78

1. There is nothing more yielding and weak on Earth than water.
2. Yet for vanquishing the hard and strong,
   nothing can better it,
   nothing can approach being its equal.
3. The weak can overcome the strong,
   the yielding can overcome the stiff-necked.
4. Everyone knows this fact,
   yet no one knows how to use it.
5. Thus I say:
   One who takes on the suffering of the people
   is fit to be a leader—
   worthy of standing before Gaia, the Barley Mother.
6. One who takes on the calamities of the people
   is a leader worthy of the name.
7. The truth often at first sounds strange.

79

1. In the dawn of new peace between old enemies,
   the haze of mistrust must be removed.
   How does one accomplish this?
2. We keep our word,
   yet do not demand our due.
3. The compassionate takes over the budget,
   the arrogant becomes head-executioner.
4. The Prime Imperative is the Soul of Equality.
   The compassionate hold to the Passage forever.

80

1. The smaller the country,
   the fewer people it can support.
2. If they arm the militias,
   they will not let them use their weapons against each other.
3. If they fear death,
   they will not make expeditions.
4. If they possess ships and war-wagons,
   they will not make use of them.
5. If they have armor and weapons,
   they will hide them.
6. Teach the people to return to innocence:
   to enjoy good, ordinary food,
   to find comfort in strong, simple clothes,
   to be content in warm, quiet homes,
   to be tranquil in way of life.
7. Though they live within sight of each other,
   and dogs' barking and roosters' crowing
   are heard through the trees,
   they will live in peace,
   and die in peace
   without ever having had a fuss.

81

1. The truth does not always seem beautiful.
   Beautiful words are often not true.
2. Good words do not always motivate.
   Moving words are not always proper.
3. The knowledgeable are often uneducated.
   The educated are often in the dark.
4. The wise One is no miser:
   having given all, even more is received.
5. Having done much, even more can be done.
6. The Passage is sharp,
   yet does not cut:
   gives benefit
   and does no harm.
7. The Passage bestows all bounty,
   and renews all bounty in return.

Rescrīpta Athenadorī

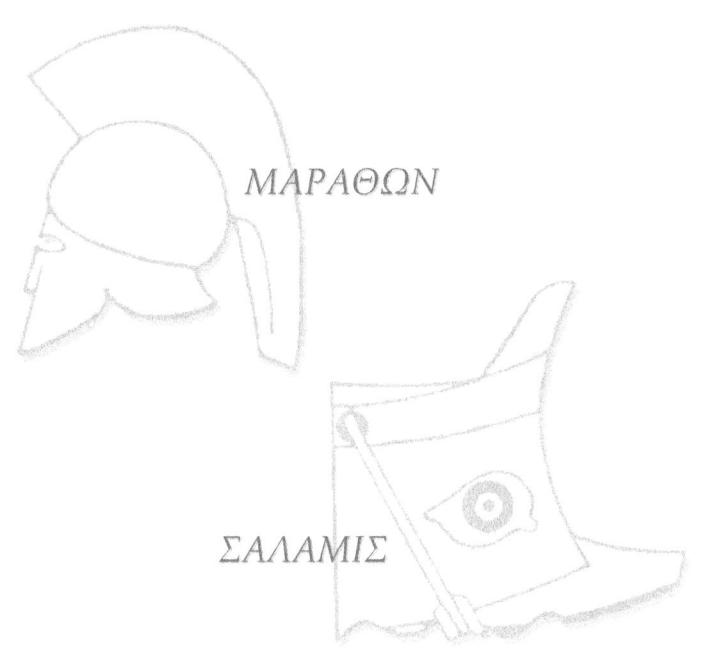

ΜΑΡΑΘΩΝ

ΣΑΛΑΜΙΣ

Homosexuality: its Genetic Basis & Evolutionary Benefit

Rescrīptum Athenadorī N° 1: In Cultūs Prænōtiōnem Generis
Rescript N° 1 of Athenadorus: Against Religious Prejudice Toward Sexuality

SCIENCE Has established that one of the most powerful influences on the behavior of living things is their drive to pass their genes on to the next, and future, generations. Many have seen in this a reason to label homosexuality as unnatural, and a further justification for making homosexuals the object of their hatred and derision.

However, this label of execration hides major flaws in the logic, facts and observations of those who use it. Not only is homosexuality natural, it bestows evolutionary benefits to the cultures in which it is allowed to function freely, in accordance with Nature's design.

HOMOSEXUALITY[1] Exists in proven ratios in all mammal species. Studies, biological and psychological,[2] have shown that homosexuality is a product of genetics, and that it is evidenced, among other things, in differences in brain structure and in individuals' responses to hormones. These structural and functional characteristics are different from those of both male and female heterosexuals. This shows that the brain of homosexuals is specialized for a particular purpose, in the same way that the brains and bodies of males and females are specialized for the roles each is, in general, to play in the future of its species. The question, the answer to which has either stumped previous investigators, or has been pointedly ignored, is this: why would evolution create and continue a situation in which it seems that genetic material is lost?

Only within the last thirty to fifty years has sufficient information been available to allow for an answer to this question.

In each cell in every complex living thing's body there are organelles called mitochondria. These mitochondria are essentially what enable multicellular life, for they are the 'refineries' in which each cell transforms the energy contained in glucose molecules into a form that the cell can use to power its activities. Without these mitochondria, cells would have no power with which to perform even the most simple tasks, much less to perform such complicated, vital things as the contraction of chemical strands to provide muscular movement.

Mitochondria contain their own DNA. This DNA is separate in origin and almost completely independent of that DNA contained in the nucleus of the cell.

All mitochondria are inherited from one's mother and only from the mother. Therefore, contrary to the view that all DNA is inherited equally from each parent, the fact is that more DNA is inherited from the mother than from the father.[3] Each child is, therefore, genetically more closely related to its mother than to its father.

Because of the pattern of inheritance of nuclear and mitochondrial DNA, there is a possibility, however slight, that a woman will be as closely related to her siblings, and to her sisters' children as she is to her own children. There also exists the possibility that a man will actually be genetically more closely related to his siblings and to his sisters' children than he will be to his own. Statistically, these possibilities are small, but, given the fact that certain genetic mixes appear to be more inheritable–as shown by the amazing similarities one sees among siblings and their children–these possibilities are reinforced by the physical and chemical properties and behaviors of the chromosomes.

The organelles and activities behind this slight difference in per-parent genetic inheritance comprise one of the most vital parts of inheritance, for mitochondrial-DNA and its expression determine the base-level viability of the animated organism. If something inherits mitochondrial-DNA that functions at higher efficiency, or that causes its cells to operate chemically more efficiently, that organism has received a survival advantage at least as great as any that its nuclear-DNA can have bestowed.

Because uncles and aunts can be as closely related to their siblings and those siblings' children as they would be to their own—or potentially, more closely related—the path of genetic information through generations is far less clearly delimited than that previously assumed by theorists. This shows that to protect one's genetic heritage it can be just as effective to make sure one's siblings and their progeny survive as it is to reproduce oneself. Indeed, for a certain number of members of a kinship group, in times of material shortage, drought, famine or war, it may actually be *more* effective.

One would expect to find that this situation has found expression in evolution, that this opportunity has been taken advantage of by evolution. Indeed, it has, in at least two different ways, depending on the complexity of the organisms involved.

The main classes of social insects—wasps, bees and ants—are all descended from primitive wasps. Primitive wasps still exist, one such species being the paper wasps of Panama. Among these primitive wasps, all the wasps in one nest are sisters. One dominates the rest: the others build the nest and gather food, but only the dominant sister lays eggs. The sisters will guard the eggs and feed the larva as if they were their own; very many, if not most, of the genes in the eggs and larvæ are common to all the sisters. Because the nest is so well guarded, and the young so better provided for, more young will survive than would if the sisters had nested singly.[4] This dedication of siblings' efforts and resources for the good of the family unit is the basis of the lives of all social insects.

Amongst the higher animals, Life expresses this benefit as homosexuality.

In what way has this evolutionary force shown itself, to perpetuate and reinforce the occurrence of homosexuality?

In early human societies, *e.g.*, those of many of the indigenous Americans, homosexual members of the tribe were accepted into their societies and fulfilled vital roles as members of their tribe. They brought to their kinship groups an increased capacity for the production of food and other essentials, and a greater ability for that group to defend itself, while at the same time they did not increase the load on the vital supplies of the group, by producing children of their own.

The benefits produced by these individuals accrued most fully to the advantage of the homosexual's siblings and of those siblings' children. Thereby, the effect of the existence of these homosexuals was to increase the survivability of those most likely to be most closely genetically related to them.

Homosexuality is an adaptation that augments the survivability of the gene pool most closely related to that individual. It is prima facie evidence that bearing offspring is not the only way Nature has developed for ensuring the passage of a majority of one's genes to future generations.

This same beneficial effect has perpetuated itself throughout the life of the human community. The most visible fulfillment has changed only slightly, in that it now more often occurs as discrete transactions and is economic in expression. When a niece or nephew inherits money from a 'bachelor' uncle, or she or he receives a legacy from a 'spinster' aunt, exactly the same process is occurring that transpired in those early human communities. The activities of that homosexual relative ultimately go to increasing the survivability of their kinship group, of the contiguous gene pool.

> "Homosexuality is a genetic biological response to the need for greater gathering and concentration of resources for the use of family- or identity-groups."[5]

This increase in the survivability of the kinship- or identity-group has only become more broad and pervasive in Western Civilization, in which homosexual members have stood as observers (look-outs, if you will) over the cultural landscape. They have absorbed that cultural experience, invigorated it, and emitted it in ever greater, ever more insightful forms, as the legacy of all members of their Civilization.

The augmentation of cultural power caused by the productivity of these homosexual members of Western society is evident from the earliest days of Classical cultures through to the present day. From Solon, Sappho and Socrates on, the turbo-charging of Western Civilization until it has become the single most dominant culture in the world is in no small way the product of the surplus of energy and insight provided by the homosexual members of this culture.

The physical and social expressions of homosexuality arise from needs and drives common to all mammals, indeed to most animals. These are the need for physical and emotional intimacy, the need for companionship, and the need for sex.[6] Merely being homosexual does not remove the needs or drives also possessed by heterosexuals—the mammalian base of human animate nature does not evaporate and is not overridden. In fact, the continued expression of these innate forces further strengthens the realization that homosexuality is indeed one of the natural expressions of sexuality. The fulfillment of those human drives for contact and companionship dramatically increases the augmentation effect. Asexuality, denial or abstention each defeat all such effects, and cannot be considered viable alternatives to animate sexuality.

Homosexuals who form pair bonds are expressing the basic human need for devoted companionship, an expression that tremendously increases their ability to gain and store resources—resources that accrue to the benefit of their families, their friends, their society. Homosexuals free to establish such relationships cross boundaries, link sensibilities and expand the knowledge and realization of other groups. Those in such relationships thereby augment the capacities and worth of their individual and combined families, their own groups, their own cultures.[7] They increase and enhance the survivability of their contiguous gene pools far more than they would if they remained isolated or if they sequestered themselves at home within their families, and did not engage in pair-bonds and in community.

I F ONE Follows the development of life from its simplest forms, one sees a progressive expansion of mental capacity and capabilities. From the simplest forms one sees a (chemical-based) recognition of *self*. In a very few amphibian and reptile species the females have expanded from the self to attain a basic awareness of offspring, an awareness which has progressed to the recognition of *family* among some birds, and which takes full root among the mammals. Only among mammals, with their advanced mental capacity, does the realization of *community* finally emerge and develop.

Homosexuality is never found among species that cannot to some degree recognize *family*. It starts to appear, but is very rare among those species that have attained the realization of family but have gone no further. Its incidence rises with increasing recognition of *community*, to the point that it is most common among those species with the greatest mental capacity: primates and cetaceans.

The appearance of homosexuality is itself a marker of the advanced mental power of a species. An attempt to denigrate its existence is, in turn, a very obvious sign of an individual's, a family's or an organization's lapse into a weak, superstitious—reptilian—mentality.

A LL The objections against homosexuality raised by male-dominated, patriarchal groups do not survive the sword of reason. Such disapproval is based on the illogic of personal prejudice, cultural backwardness, on religious superstition: fear, hatred and ignorance.

Some of the more unenlightened members of modern society have said that homosexuality is a disease, "like alcoholism". This is patently false. Homosexuality exists without external impetus; it exists without the introduction of foreign chemicals and without the infliction of external actions by others.

Others have said that it is a genetic 'predisposition', "like lying and stealing". This is utter nonsense. It exists in animal species in which these actions—these "sins"—cannot occur.[8] Unlike lying and stealing, homosexuality endows specific, long-term benefits. It is as natural as blue eyes, left-handedness, or the genetic predisposition to walk on two legs.

Religious objections to homosexuality spring from two sources. One is the ancient patriarchal warrior-clan religion on which several modern religions are based. In their primitive clans it was every male's duty to breed, to produce more soldiers, and any who didn't were violating cult taboo: it was taken as a sign of non-male weakness, of "sin" against their warrior Father.

The other source of these cultic condemnations has been the need of religious and political leaders, who, in trying to force their religion and its observance on the peoples of their communities, have created mythic polemics that attempt to denigrate and destroy the religious beliefs and practices of others. This is the origin of the myth of Sodom and Gomorrah, and of the opprobrious dicta of Saul/Paul.

Because denial of the rights and safety of homosexuals is based solely on religion, **all hate crimes committed against homosexuals are crimes of religion. Each denial of homosexual rights is the illegal establishment of religion over and above the rights of the individual.**

AS ALL Objections against homosexuality are purely religious in origin, expression and purpose, they must be relegated to the cults and mythologies from which they derive. They have no place in a logical, scientific, psychologically healthy life. They have no place in public law.

ATHENADORUS

[1] *Homosexuality* is that aspect of nature distinguished by the direction of the pair-bonding* impetus toward members of the same sex. This differentiates it from that state in which the pair-bonding impetus is directed toward the opposite sex, the state termed *heterosexuality*. These are the two *genders* of animate life.**

In using the terms *heterosexuality* and *homosexuality*, one must differentiate between individual sexual acts and the gender of the individual at issue. People who would, without hesitation, describe themselves as being of one particular gender often will have experimented with, or may occasionally enjoy forays into the sexual activities associated with the opposite gender.

In the ferociously anti-gay years of the past it was not uncommon for a gay man to marry a woman and produce children, as a protective 'smoke screen'. Such heterosexual activities do not change a gay man's gender, nor is it evidence that gender can be forced to change. It simply demonstrates that sexual function, sexual activity, and fertility, are not delimited by gender.

In the same way, abstention from sexuality, or from sexual acts, neither removes nor redefines gender.

Certain religious hierarchies have tried to invent and enforce a rift between gender and sexual activity. This is unnatural: whether the emotional side of a gender is expressed sexually does not redefine gender, or one's degree of 'belonging to' one's gender. Such an attitude is emotionally dangerous, psychologically damaging. It is the working of groundless ignorance: it betrays either a vapid attempt to reclaim lost religious market share by perpetually redefining "sin", or a poorly disguised attempt to protect their scriptures and dogma by perpetuating murderous, gender-based hatred.

Abstention from sexuality, or from sexual acts, neither removes nor redefines gender in and of itself.

---

* [*Pair-bonding* encompasses both physical and emotional bonding.]

**[Although there are those who find members of both sexes to be sexually appealing, or who have sexual or emotional relations with both males and females within the same general period, even these will come to live within, and to identify themselves as members principally of, one of these two genders. That is, one who describes his or her activities or attitude as 'bisexual' will in fact live either alone or within a pair-bond of one of the specific genders, and will merely bring into this situation others that fulfill these emotional needs and sexual desires.

Human attempts at three-member emotional/sexual units, *ménages à trois*, are inherently unstable. This is because of the ease with which one of the three can come to feel excluded or slighted, and because with three individuals, there tends to be one who gets emotionally 'in the middle', and who thereby distances the other two from each other. True long-term three-partner emotional/sexual situations are so rare and fragile that they cannot be taken to provide enough evidence of a true third gender.

Bisexuality in fact describes the continuum between, and the interaction of, the two genders, and although it is a real and valid self-description, it is not a gender in and of itself.]

[2] Studies and publications such as those of:

psychologist Michael Bailey of Northwestern University and psychiatrist Richard C. Pillard of Boston (1992-93)

neuroscientists Laura Allen and Roger Gorski, UCLA School of Medicine (1992)
neurologist Simon LeVay, Salk Institute for Biological Studies, San Diego (1992)
psychiatrist Sandra Witelson, McMaster University, Hamilton, Ontario (1994)
biologist and researcher Bruce Bagemihl: *Biological Exuberance; Animal Homosexuality and Natural Diversity*, Profile Books, London: 1999 [978-1-861-971-82-1].
psychologist Anthony F. Bogaert, Brock University, St. Catharines, Ontario (2006).

[3] The nucleus of each cell receives about 3,000,000,000 DNA base-pairs from each parent. Each loop of mitochondrial DNA contains only 16,569 base pairs. [*Scientific American*; August 1997, p. 42] However, because each mitochondrion contains tens of these loops of DNA, and each cell contains thousands to hundreds of thousands of mitochondria, the actual average number of mitochondrial-DNA base pairs per cell can be estimated at something around 170,000,000. This represents one full percent of all genetic material present in the cell: material required for the life of that cell.

Because all mitochondrial DNA is inherited from the female parent, the percentages of contribution would therefore be approximately 48.6% from the male parent, 51.4% from the female. Yet the percentage of that inherited from the female is greatly increased due to the fact that so much of the nuclear DNA is structural, repetitive or otherwise nonfunctional: **only about 3% of the 3 billion DNA base-pairs actually code viable proteins**. Any active coding regions in the remaining base-pairs encode regulatory RNA molecules. [*The Cell*; Geoffrey M. Cooper; ASM Press 1997, p. 143.]

This means that the total number of protein-encoding DNA base pairs inherited from each parent is only around 90,000,000. This state contrasts with the fact that essentially all the mitochondrial DNA is functional. The result of this is that **around 60% of all protein-encoding DNA is received from the mother, and about 40% from the father**.

The mechanism that insures the paternal mitochondria are destroyed is that they are tagged with the protein that flags intracellular structures for 'recycling': *ubiquitin*. After fertilization has occurred, the processes of the successfully engendered embryo destroy those mitochondria bearing that tag. This leaves only the c. 100,000 maternal mitochondria of the egg. These mitochondria have demonstrated that their communication link with the nucleus itself is sound—else the mother would not have survived to have produced the ovum itself. Embryos that are not able to delete the paternal mitochondria do not survive. ["Mom's eggs execute Dad's mitochondria", *Science News*, Vol. 157, No. 1, p. 5; January 1, 2000.]

[4] Paraphrased and extended from David Attenborough, "Life in the Undergrowth", broadcast on Animal Planet television network, April 30, 2006.

[5] Athenadorus, *The Athenadoran Library; The Danaa* §XV. Danaan Press 2011.

[6] The "need for physical and emotional intimacy, the need for companionship" are for most animals subsumed within, and subordinated to, the need for sex.

But even with this said, one should guard against the Victorian, conservative prejudice that sex is for procreation only. For our nearest biological relatives, the bonobos, or pygmy chimpanzees, even more than among humans, sex is far more than merely the mechanical transferal of sperm into proximity with egg.

The activities of the Whiptail lizards of the American Southwest give further support to holding that sex is more than merely spermatic transfer. This species of lizards has no males: all the members are females who give birth to female copies of themselves. However, even though they have no need for sex—indeed they cannot have *heterosexual* sex—they continue to exhibit 'sexual' mating behavior.

The fact that they continue to engage in this mating behavior shows that they are still involved in sexual selection. Those who are not in an acceptable breeding state will not be able to attract a partner with which to 'mate'. This reduced acceptability will most likely have been the result, if not of unluck, of spontaneous or environmentally induced genetic changes in those individuals.

The puzzling effect of their 'mating' activity is that those lizards that engage in homosexual mating actually produce more eggs, and the eggs they produce are healthier, stronger and more likely to hatch successfully than those who don't 'mate'. Thus any lizard that cannot attract a partner will be much reduced in its ability to produce viable offspring, and this resulting reduced fertility will accrue to the benefit of the species. (An interesting point proved by this activity is that the genetic directions for male courtship activities and sexual movements do not reside on the Y chromosome, but are present in the female genome common to females and males.)

The physical, psychological and social aspects that surround the achieving of sexual pleasure, in whichever sexuality or expression their achievement may be couched, are in many ways as important for the welfare of a species as is the physical act of fertilization. For without the supporting guarantees bestowed by these auxiliary activities and qualities, the eventual result of fertilization would most often be failure.

[7] Anyone who would claim that the augmentation imperative even hints that homosexuals would better serve their contiguous gene pools by staying sequestered within the family unit and "babysitting their nephews and nieces" has little understanding of the synergistic effect of gay relationships, and is unfortunately unaware of just how drastically these relationships multiply the benefits accruing to their communities.

As we know that the most important influence on business success is the building of a personal networking web, one can also say this, with equal aptness, of personal and connubial success.

[8] To assert that animals can commit sin means that they must also have souls—for only those with souls are capable of "moral" (or "immoral") action. This is contrary to the teachings of the extant patriarchal cults, as having a soul is a right reserved by them for humans alone.

THE BIOLOGY OF RELATEDNESS: GENETICS, STATISTICS & THE STINGY GENE

EACH Human cell contains 46 chromosomes in its nucleus. When the egg and sperm combine to create another human, each of those two brings a set of 23 chromosomes from either parent. Each chromosome is one from the pair of chromosomes that parent had received from its parents. At first sight, this mixing of sources might imply a very high degree of variability, as the number of sets of 23 that can be drawn from the chromosomes involved is 8,388,608[1].

However, because chimpanzees and bonobos[2] share more than 98% of our (nuclear) genetic material, less than 2% of that variation must account for the characteristics of being human. Because of the structure of chromosomes, 97% of those must involve structural, or non-functional, genes.[3] So, fewer than 5033 chromosomal variations-worth of genetic differentiation would account for all that it means to be human. This is not unreasonable in view of the enormous number of genes involved, for the vast majority of those must be static across our species. Otherwise, odd body arrangements, vastly unusual chemical products and sequences, extraordinary colors and behaviors would regularly appear at random amongst the human population, indeed amongst all species. This simply does not happen: the overwhelming majority of genes must code for the basic processes of life. Humans digest plant matter in the same chemical way cows do; human muscles are physically constructed identically to and work in the same way and from the same control mechanisms as those of earthworms and frogs. The relatively few genes left over are those that must code for those things that separate us from our nearest relatives, the bonobos and chimpanzees.

Two percent of the 46 chromosomes averages out to just less than one chromosome, actually 0.92 chromosome. Thus, mathematically, the

---

[1] 8,388,608 = [Combination(2,1)]^23: each parental chromosome is one taken randomly from the two each parent inherited from her or his parents; each member of the set of 23 can appear as either of those two, creating that number of possible variations. (There are two choices for chromosome 1; four choices possible for chromosomes 1 & 2 taken together; eight ways of choosing chromosomes 1 & 2 & 3 at the same time; 16 ways of arranging chromosomes 1 through 4 at the same time; and so forth up to 23. For a child's chromosomes from both parents the number of possible arrangements is 70,368,744,177,664.)

[2] Bonobos were formerly called *pygmy chimpanzees*. See "Bonobo Sex and Society", *Scientific American*, Vol. 272, No. 3 (March 1995), pp. 82-8.

genetic composition of a single chromosome is enough to make us humans, and not bonobos. This means that the genetic information shared amongst siblings must, by default, be extremely similar, if it is not, in fact, very nearly identical. If it did not maintain its family or species identity, we would have other family, other species, characteristics appearing at random among groups of siblings. Because this does not happen, we may say with reassurance that the percentage of identical genetic information shared among siblings is relatively very high.

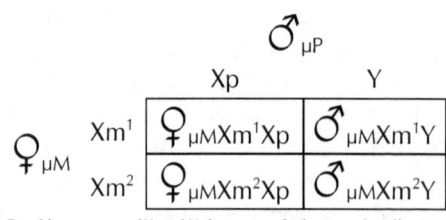

Possible sequences of X- and Y-chromosomal inheritance by offspring.

Part of the relatively small amount of genetic material that establishes the individual is carried on the sex-specific chromosomes. Because of this, and because these are the most widely known chromosomes, they are used in the following graphs. Although they are used specifically, they may also be seen to represent that small amount of nuclear genetic material whose effects are those that establish the species-specific effects leading to humans.

The following graphs portray the most highly exaggerated case, in which the chromosomes of each parent remain distinct and are passed to their offspring as a unit. They portray the extremes: both most related and least related possibilities in each scenario are revealed on the same diagram. To keep the charts simple, the offspring listed in generations γ and δ are limited to 2 females and 2 males. The chromosomes each receives are indicated as unique, as delineated by the four 'canonical' possibilities given in the X- and Y-chromosome inheritance chart given above.

Although such arrangements implying that the chromosomes of common source are more likely to progress into the gamete together are not *highly* likely, they are not at all impossible. Indeed, the physical, anecdotal, evidence is that some genes seem to be more mobile, or more chemically 'enthusiastic', so that they are the ones most likely to be passed on to egg or sperm. It is easily discernible how much alike most brothers and sisters look and act. Although this may be an expression of statistical probability, it may also reflect the more engenderable nature of certain patterns of (parental) chromosomes.

Along with this, the quite often extremely similar physiques and activity-patterns of siblings are an obvious and unmistakable manifestation of the all-pervading effects of their shared, identical maternal mitochondrial DNA.

For most people, this pattern of genetic inheritance is a matter of statistical probability. But for the children of identical twins, it is absolute: the identical twin children of identical twin sisters are as closely related to their aunt as they are to their mother. Identical twin children of identical twin fathers, though as closely related to their father as they are to his brother, are not genetically as closely related to either of them as they are to their mother, for it is only her mitochondrial DNA that they possess.

Legend for the following charts:

μM = *maternal mitochondrial DNA*
μP = *paternal mitochondrial DNA*

Xm^1 = *maternal nuclear-DNA, set 1*
Xp = *paternal nuclear-DNA, set 1, containing X-chromosome*
Xm^2 = *maternal nuclear-DNA, set 2*
Y = *paternal nuclear-DNA, set 2, containing Y-chromosome*

Subscripted Greek letters refer to the generation in which that genetic material was introduced into the lineages portrayed in these graphs.

Underlining:
Double underlines indicate example-flow of maternal DNA of the individual of interest in generation γ, from generation α throughout the chart.

Offspring of daughter, ♀γ2 [♀μM¹α Xm²α Xpα]**:**

Generation:

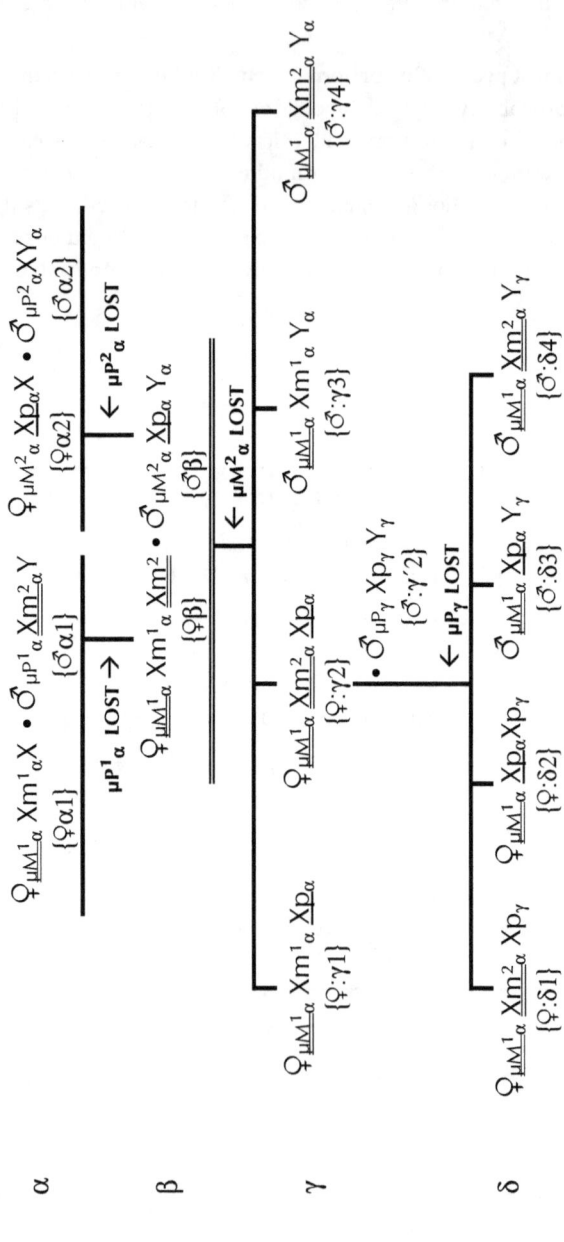

Shared Genetic Material (Sex chromosomes & mitochondrial DNA)

Generation δ Member →		♀:δ1	♀:δ2	♂:δ3	♂:δ4
Generation γ Member (aunt & uncles)	♀:γ1	— μDNA	≤ 50% m-DNA μDNA	≤ 50% m-DNA μDNA	— μDNA
	♂:γ3	— μDNA	— μDNA	— μDNA	— μDNA
	♂:γ4	≤ 50% m-DNA μDNA	— μDNA	— μDNA	≤ 50% m-DNA μDNA
Children of mother	♀:γ2	50% DNA μDNA	50% DNA μDNA	50% DNA μDNA	50% DNA μDNA
Children of father	♂:γ'2	50% DNA	50% DNA	50% DNA	50% DNA

"—" means essentially no shared maternal or paternal DNA

This shows that, on an extrapolated average, in 50% of cases, there exists some possibility that an aunt will be as closely genetically related to her sisters' children as she is to her own children.

This also reveals that in 25% of the situations, there is a possibility that an uncle will be as closely related to his sisters' children as he is or would be to his own.

Aunts and uncles always possess the same mitochondrial DNA as the children of their sisters.

Offspring of son, ♂γ1 [♂μM¹α Xm¹α Y α]:

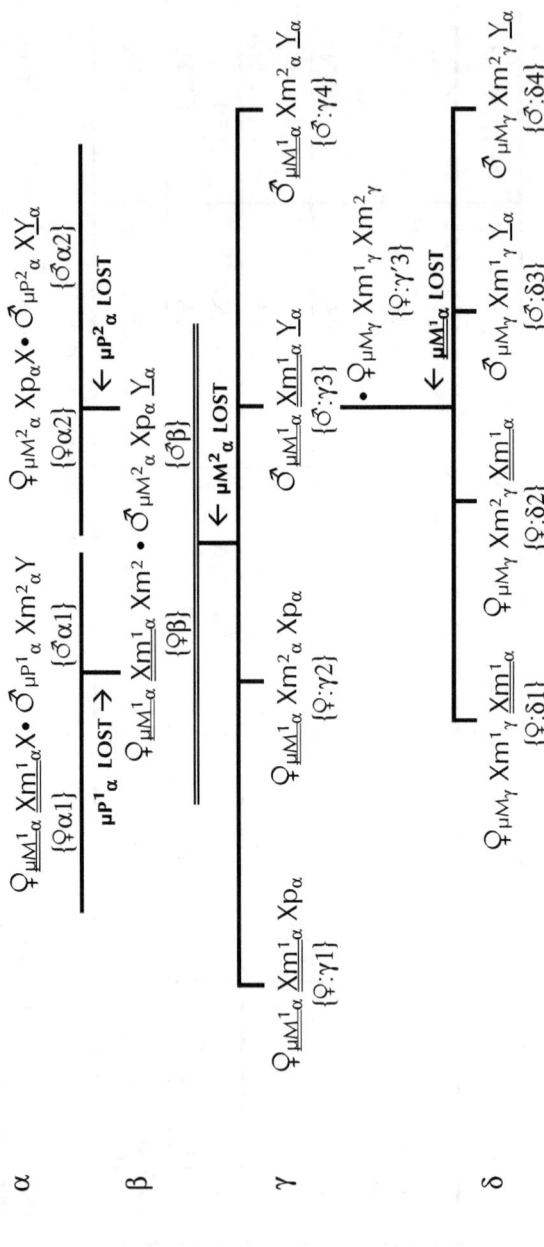

Shared Genetic Material (Sex chromosomes & mitochondrial DNA)

Generation δ Member →		♀:δ1	♀:δ2	♂:δ3	♂:δ4
Generation γ Member (aunts & uncle)	♀:γ1	≤ 50% m-DNA	≤ 50% m-DNA	—	—
	♀:γ2	—	—	—	—
	♂:γ4	—	—	≤ 50% m-DNA	≤ 50% m-DNA
Children of mother	♀:γ3	50% DNA μDNA	50% DNA μDNA	50% DNA μDNA	50% DNA μDNA
Children of father	♂:γ3	50% DNA	50% DNA	50% DNA	50% DNA

"—" means essentially no shared maternal or paternal DNA

This chart indicates that, on an extrapolated average, in 25% of cases there exists a possibility that an aunt will be as closely genetically related to her brother's children as she is to her own children. However, this does not include the mitochondrial DNA, which she does not share with the offspring of her male siblings.

This also imparts the fact that in 50% of the cases the possibility of close relation exists between uncle and nephews, while there is virtually no chance that an uncle will be as closely related to his brothers' daughters as he is or would be to his own.

Because of the inheritance pattern of mitochondrial DNA, in absolute terms of functional DNA, no father is genetically as closely related to his children as those children are to their mother. Yet, even at this, they are *his* children; and his responsibility toward them—and his joy and benefit from them—is no less than that of their mother.

ATHENADORUS

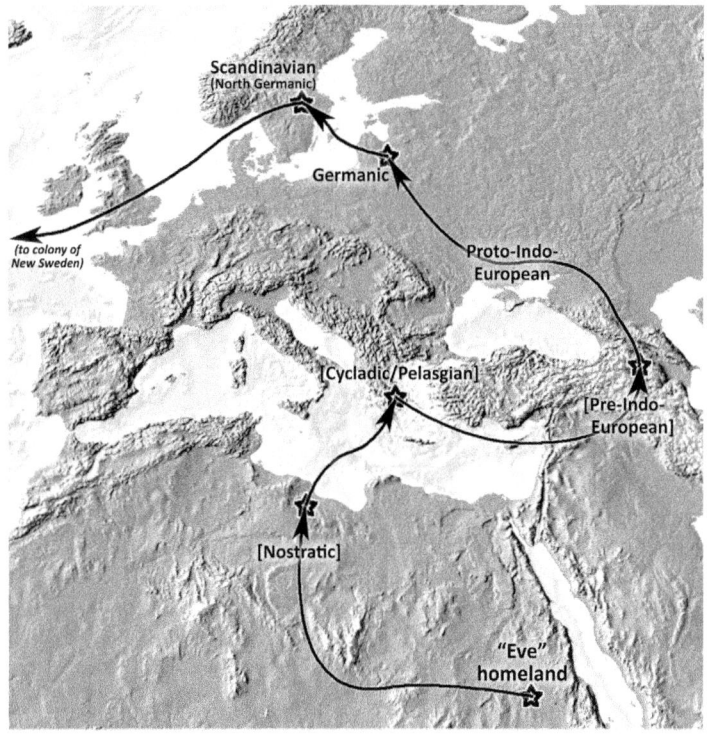

An example of the historical linearity of mitochondrial DNA inheritance:
The *c.* 225,000 year odyssey of Athenadorus's mitochondria from the African source of all human mitochondria up to their journey to the New World *c.* EY 5.2652 [1630].

Names in brackets are suggestions of the linguistic and/or cultural affiliations of the groups in the areas in which the mitochondria were extant.
["Nostratic" is the suggested mother language of both the Indo-european and the Afro-asiatic (Semitic and Hamitic) language groups; "Pre-Indo-european" is the suggested mother of the Indo-european and the Anatolian (Hittite, Luvian, etc.) language families.]

The Female: First Form
& Source of Life

Rescrīptum Athenadorī N° 2: In Cultūs Prænōtiōnem Mulieribus
Rescript N° 2 of Athenadorus: Against Religious Prejudice Toward Women

ꝑe mayle doth, yea, produce the ſeede compleate: the femayle meerely broodeth hys creatioun untill it be of a ſize ſurvivable. For, having enticed hym into that most injuryous damnatioun of the ſinn originall, perpetuall bee her ſhame and puniſhment to have to carrye the chyldrenn he doth produce, and to deliver them unto hym in paine and anguiſh, that do cauſe eternall remembraunce thereto of her noxious and moſt heinous ſinn. She is a moste weake, emptie and incompleate veſſel untill the mayle doth beſtowe of hys owne goddly fertilitie uponn her.

The mayle was created the forme originall, beinge the truest image of thys, hys God. The femayle was mayde only ſecondarilie from him, after his compleate, divyne originatioun, that she bee hys veray ſervaunt, and uponn whom he ſhall begett hys ſons.

Thus is the nature of reproduction portrayed in the mythology of the father-god cults. It is incorrect. It is wrong. It is damnably false.

All living things begin their development as immature females of their species. No matter what DNA mix it carries, every fetus begins its life with the form of the female. **The female is the original, not the male.**

It is easy to see why the error of male pre-eminence arose. It is the male that produces a substance external and unusual, clearly associated with reproduction, whereas the female generates no such obvious material: the female appears an empty vessel. From the male's production of that visible substance, the analogy arose that the male was doing exactly that act performed by farmers, that is, he was placing complete, fully viable seed into a temporary, enclosing environment for its intermediate development. But this analogy is false, absolutely false.

That substance visibly contributed by the male transfers half of the DNA necessary for the full functioning of the nuclear DNA of the cells that will become a new individual of its species. This one-half of the nuclear DNA is the entire contribution the male makes to the physical conception of this new life. It is vitally important, yet the emphasis placed on it as the end-all, be-all of procreation has been so profoundly exaggerated as to have become absurd–it has perverted the laws, attitudes and structures of human society.

The contribution the female makes to this new life is far greater than that allotted to the male. In addition to the remaining half of the nuclear DNA, there are several structures, processes and chemicals that the female builds into the egg, thus into all the cells, of the new individual. These objects are wholly contributed by the female. They never come from the male parent: it is physically impossible.

The egg is, in fact, a cell of the mother's body, a cell from which half of the nuclear DNA has been omitted during its process of becoming an *egg* cell. In its internal organization, messages, structures, and functions, it is exactly like the other cells of the mother. Among these maternal substances, objects and processes, the most important are the mitochondria; the ribosomes and their associated RNA's; and disease-fighting chemicals, the immuno-globulins.[1]

The fetus is bathed in the immuno-globulins suffused into the womb from the fluids of the mother's body. These substances persist for some time in the newborn, as its initial, primary disease-fighting capacity.

The maternal ribosomes and RNA's made available to the embryo allow it to grow until it has reached a size and complexity that permit it to replace them with those of its own production.

However, of those specific three inherited from the mother, the most persistently important are the mitochondria. The mitochondria convert the energy contained in the chemical bonds of glucose molecules into an intermediate form that can be safely and easily moved about the cell itself, then released when and where needed to power those chemical reactions necessary for the life of the cell.

Mitochondria contain their own DNA, DNA unrelated to that located in the nucleus of the cell. This non-nuclear, genetic material controls the nature and efficiency of the chemical reactions mediated by the mitochondria, as well as the reproduction of the mitochondria themselves. The DNA of the cell's nucleus contains no instructions for making mitochondria: *only a mitochondrion can produce mitochondria.*

Those mitochondria bestowed by the mother are the only ones the child will ever receive. They will replicate themselves with every cell division until they are contained in each living cell of the child's body, to power all tasks necessary in the body. And they will continue this replication and empowerment throughout the child's existence.

Life as we know it is impossible without mitochondria.

Yet *all* mitochondria are inherited from the mother and *only* from the mother.[2]

The sexual form of an individual is determined by its sex chromosomes. For mammals in particular, two X-chromosomes are present in the female; one X-chromosome and a Y-chromosome exist in the male.

However, in females one of those two X-chromosomes is non-functional; it shrivels into what is called a *Barr body*. Because of this, females are actually creatures of one X-chromosome.[3]

Males are also creatures with only one X-chromosome. Their Y-chromosome (that takes the "place" of the Barr body) causes few processes other than those necessary to change the original one-X-chromosome form—the female—into that other, one-X-chromosome form, the form that we recognize as the male.

The Y-chromosome is that which was added by evolutionary processes to create the male from the female.

While the XY-chromosome fetus is in the womb it will, under normal circumstances, undergo two surges of hormonal activity that result in the development of the fully formed XY-individual. These chemical fluxes do not occur in the development of the female, the XX-individual: they exist only in the maturation process of the male fetus.

The first set of hormones stops the production of fully-formed female sexual characteristics. This is required because the functional X-chromosome of both males and females contains complete instructions for molding the fetus into a female form, a process that will continue automatically if not interrupted. To produce a 'canonical' male form, these genes must be switched off, by the chemical action of hormones, before the second surge of chemicals is allowed to arise.

That second group of hormones sets in motion the production of male sexual characteristics.

The existence of these two hormonal surges explains the presence among structurally normal-chromosome'd XY-individuals of sexual neuters, hermaphrodites and Y-chromosome-females. In hermaphrodites, the first surge does not occur; in neuters, the second surge does not occur; in Y-chromosome-females, neither surge occurs.

The male never loses those female structures and characteristics it starts out with, the most obvious example being his nipples. All male sexual characteristics are derived from female structures: the male has no parts that do not exist in their original form in the female.

Many young men, while watching the changes worked on them by the metamorphosis of puberty, discover a 'suture' line running along the center axis of the scrotum, continuing up along the underside of the penis.[4] They do not realize that this scar is the line along which what had been their original, external female organs came together to form their male structures. That suture line marks where their labia fused in the process of forming the penis and the scrotum. **Contrary to the biblically derived idea that the female is a male with no penis, the truth is actually that *the male is a female with an adapted vulva*.**

When that second surge of hormones flows through the body of the XY-fetus, those structures that had just previously been made to stop developing into ovaries start to descend from their original ovary-positions, down and out through the body wall into the pouch the body has simultaneously been creating from part of what had been the fetus's labia.

The descent of the gonads from their ovary-positions into the developing scrotum is inherently a destructive process. It requires that the incipient testicles push their way through the musculo-tendinous membranes of the body cavity to reach the outside. Because these membranes have already formed in a way that is female-specific in how they reinforce and support the internal organs, this pushing of the testicles through them creates weaknesses in those membranes.[5] This is the reason males can so easily develop hernias in this area: the external testicles are, in fact, already a herniation.[6]

In retelling the several myths that he combined to create the biblical myth of Noah, the editor of that text has Yava commanding Noah to take, in one verse[7], two of each animal–one male and one female, and in other verses[8] , seven pairs of each "clean" animal and two of each "unclean" of each beast "the male and his female". Among other observations[9] it is very interesting that this creator god has forgotten that there are several species of animals–species that he is supposed to have created specifically and separately–in which there are no males.[10] In these species, the females produce eggs that are already fertile–no male input is necessary, nor, indeed, is it possible, for **there are no males in those species**.

There are several species of fish in which all offspring are born female. On the occurrence of certain environmental stimuli, some of the females of these species will, from hormonal actions, turn into males.[11]

Although there are fish species that bear hermaphroditic offspring, capable of shifting between male-functionality and female-functionality, there are no species, fish or otherwise, that produce only male offspring.

The female is the original form of life: the male is the second form, generated from that original form in each instance.

The mythology that holds that the male is the original, true form has been used for many thousands of years as false evidence of the divinely ordained superiority of the male. It has been cited as legitimization of man's abuse of woman. From denial of rights to rape to murder, this lie has been perpetrated against her.

Because man has so long preached that woman is incompletely developed—imperfect in body, mind and spirit—she has long been treated as inferior.

Few realize today that up until around a hundred years ago, in many parts of the United States a woman could not own property in her own name. In most regions, all property a young woman's father held for her was transferred, at marriage, not to her, but to her husband. If her husband died, her eldest son took her into tutelage. Thus she was passed from male domination to male domination.

The assumption of male pre-eminence has caused the work of woman to be undervalued, her role in society to be ignored, her effects on history to be dismissed.

Because the male is merely a form derived from the female original, he is indeed still female. Male violence against women is a depraved expression of his own, societally inflicted self-hatred.

This perverted condition arose in its most heinous form and enforcement in the late days of the Roman Empire. Having begun with Constantine's imposition of a misogynist, gynophobic religion, constantly reinforced through the inventions of the Dark Ages, and continuing to this day, the disempowerment of woman has been horribly, viciously, violently enforced.

This violence must now end.

The male is not superior to the female, nor is she superior to him. She is the source. He is its companion. She is the font of the great Waters of Life. He is the one whose swimming helps keep those waters alive. We are all one species.

Sexuality is a continuum, an arch o'er-reaching the sexes. It unites all peoples in our one, full purpose: the peaceful enrichment of the burgeoning lives of all humans.

We are each gifted as individuals, endowed by our birth with unique skills and strengths. Yet these gifts of the Earth, our ultimate mother, cannot be fully and freely made use of until we are all free.

That heinous misunderstanding, the sanctified vilification of the female is unnatural. That too-long list of acts of bias, of bigotry, of violence against women cries out, the unsilenceable witness of terror perpetuated by fear, by greed and by ignorance. We must commit ourselves to removing that ignorance, to quenching that greed, to ending that fear.

All attitudes, all doctrines, all institutions that propagate this mistake of male primacy, who perpetuate the perversion of male-specific creation, birth or re-birth, must yield to the truth of the female source, or be destroyed by the truth.

As the female is the true, original form of life, Woman's Rights are the bulwark, the source, the very foundation of all Human Rights. Only when Woman is allowed Her full measure of Freedom will Her Children, all Her People, be vouchsafed their true Liberty.

ATHENADORUS

[1] Athenadorus, *The Athenadoran Library*; *The Danaa* §VI, Items 1-3. Danaan Press 1982, 1996, 2005.

[2] The statistical study reported in the Proceedings of the Royal Society B (vol. 266, p. 485) detailing a genetic defect present in a tiny population (on the island of Nguna in the Vanuatu archipelago, and in other geographically extremely isolated populations) merely shows the presence of a defect in nuclear DNA which causes these individuals to produce faulty copies of *ubiquitin*, the enzyme that tags alien DNA [and other objects] for destruction (a chemical discovery detailed by Sutovsky & Schatten in a presentation at the American Society for Cell Biology, 1998/12). It does not in any way diminish the statement that all mitochondrial DNA is inherited from the mother. (The statistical reports provided in 'Proceedings' were limited in their details and data.)

[3] Individuals with only one X chromosome (and neither an X or Y chromosome paired with it) are designated as "X0" individuals. In Medicine, this is called *Turner Syndrome*; it affects approximately 1 in every 2500 live births worldwide. Turner Syndrome results in an individual with the features of a female who never sexually matures.

However, it is not merely the sexual organs that never mature, there are several organ-systems that may not reach maturity in those who have this syndrome. The most severe feature can be major heart defects, for the cardiac system is one particularly important system that their bodies may not develop to a fully functional stage.

The reason for this failure is that there are a certain number of *autosomal* (non-sex related) genes that have migrated to the X and Y chromosomes in humans. In XY individuals both copies of these are always exposed, and in XX individuals the second copy of these genes is not hidden within the *Barr body*, but remains exposed, protruding from it—only the sex genes must be masked within the *Barr body* to guarantee hormonal balance. (*The variation in severity of concomitant systemic malformations is dependent on the degree to which any autosomal genes of the non-sex related, chromosomes have crossed over to the X and/or Y chromosomes. [Another example of chromosomes crossing to the X or Y chromosomes is found in cats, in which the gene for fur color has crossed to the X chromosome, producing female-only calicos.]*)

In contrast, any fertilization that results in an embryo with a Y0 set of genes (*i.e.*, no X chromosome) cannot develop, and such an embryo will be spontaneously aborted, simply because the Y chromosome does not possess the genes required to form a living body. **All fetuses must first be formed as immature females by the genes on the X chromosome, or life is not possible.**

[4] This "suture line" is separately formed from, though usually continuous with, the other obvious suture-like scar that goes from the genitalia to the anus, and which is present in some way on all vertebrates (and which is especially visible on hairless mammals). This line is formed earlier in the development of the embryo to seal the "bottom" end of the fold that becomes the tube of the digestive system.

[5] This occurs quite late in fetal development: for humans, it is often not completed until the seventh month of gestation.

[6] The processes involved are essentially these (keeping in mind that *all structure names should be prefixed with "proto-", or "the developing ..."*):

- The **gonads** move from their original, ovary-specific positions, forward and down, push through the body wall and descend in front of the **symphysis pubis** into the sack prepared by the 'suturing' of the **external labia**, *i.e.* the **scrotum**, where they are modified to become the **testes**.
- The **Wolffian duct** is extended with the travelling gonads to form the **vas deferens**, for the transport of sperm from the **testicles** after puberty. In males, testosterone forces destruction of the **Müllerian duct** (the original oviduct), causing it to disintegrate completely.

  In females the upper portion of the **Wolffian duct** simply converts into connective tissue [from lack of further development] and the lower portion melds with the forming **vagina**: the **Wolffian duct** was originally the exit pathway of fluids produced by the **mesonephric kidney**. The **Wolffian duct** in its original form is no longer needed by the female so it is simply ignored or recycled. However, the male's body must specifically remove the **Müllerian duct** physically in order to effect the complete "replumbing" of its original, female-specific system.
- The **vasa deferentia** meet in the **prostate**, made from what had started forming as the body of the **uterus**, the **cervix** and **vagina**. Within the **prostate**, the pathways leading to the outside are made to change from the female's three-exit system to the male's two-exit form by the joining of the **ducti deferentia** with the female's **ureter**, creating the male's combined pathway, the **urethra**.

  The *uterus* is not completely revamped: every male retains cellular remnants of his original *uterus*, within and upon the *prostate*.
- The **clitoris** extends forward to form the **glans** and one of the internal structures of the **penis**, the **corpus cavernosum**, around which the **internal labia** have come together to form both the body of the **penis**, and the **urethra** passing through it, which extends to exit through a fold in the **glans** (or 'head') of the **penis**, the remaining external portion of the extended **clitoris**; all of which is covered by layers of skin formed from the **external labia**.
- The sexual-pleasure nerves formed in the early vagina are retained when it is converted into the male's prostate. Because of this, the male is capable of experiencing the equivalent of both the clitoral and vaginal orgasms of the female.

This description is a general, highly non-specific list of independent structural changes. These separate processes do not happen sequentially, but progress relatively in tandem.

[7] from the earlier, 40-day flood myth

[8] from the later, 1-year flood myth

[9] such as the problem of how Noah would have gone about choosing *which* particular female was "*his* female" of the male of animals that are "polygamous", such as lions, seals, walruses, or of animals that do not form permanent pairs (which is the vast majority).

[10] Species such as the whiptail lizards of the American Southwest.

[11] For a more in-depth treatment of the complexities of the sex of fish, see "Fishy Sex; Uncovering the wild ways of fish" by Tina Adler, *Science News*, Vol. 148, No. 17, October 21, 1995, pp. 266-7.

The Male Liberated: Expanding Rôles in the Realm of Life
Rescrīptvm Athenadorī N° 3: Prō Lībertāte Virvm
Rescript N° 3 of Athenadorus: Toward the Liberation of Men

Exaltation of the male, reinforced by unquestioned domination and unrelenting denigration of the female, is the basis of the religio-social view that has been forced on Western life for the past 1600 years. He has been portrayed as the pinnacle of creation; She has been that belief's weak-brained, frail-bodied target of blame for all its own self-declared, self-deceived, "ills of humanity".

These attitudes are not natural. They are damnable in their deleterious effects on the freedom, capability and prospects of *all* Humanity.

Just as importantly, these opinions have been used as excuse for limiting the roles, attitudes and potential of the male—restricting him to those few conditions that would enforce those very limited views of human mental, emotional and ethical capacity.

The Danaan Male is unfettered by those artificial limits on human expression. He is self-assuredly dedicated to the fulfillment of his personal responsibility, and to the manner and effects of that fulfillment. If there is such a thing as "honor" for a male, it is surely that dedication and that fulfillment.

Although those general, basic qualities and opportunities of females have been expressed in other of our texts, one may still find oneself asking, What of the male? If the female is the original form, possessed of demonstrable biological qualities and physical, emotional and economic opportunities, what then is the basis for fulfillment in the life of the male?

One cannot spend more than a few minutes in human company—or, indeed in troop with any mammal—without recognizing that the vast majority of males are almost consumed by their interest in the females around them.

On a biological, evolutionary level, we see that She is the center around which the life of the male is physically designed to revolve. Because the female ultimately controls the reproductive destiny of all species, males' immediate and continual interest in the female provides her with choices: the opportunity to optimize the timing and availability of the resources that will amplify the natural success of her species, according to her schedule, her needs.

One cannot but see, as well, that when a human male establishes a successful bond with a female, his life is irrevocably—and almost always extremely positively—transformed. It is recognition of this transformation that leads us to see what is the true source of meaning in the life of the heterosexual male.

The Male finds his life-purpose in the love and devotion he expresses toward his partner, both towards her physically, and towards any new life and liveliness she bestows on their shared existence. His sense of fulfillment grows directly from the emotional, physical and economic talents he brings into the relationship, the amount and quality in which they are appreciated, and the cumulative effects generated from these interactions of their lives.

The degree to which a male may allow his existence to be intertwined—even dominated—by his desire to please his mate is his own, individual decision. For his personal welfare, he must retain ultimate control over and responsibility for his own physical and emotional well-being, just as his partner must hers. But this having been said, if it is his desire to dedicate his existence to eliciting the physical pleasure of his mate, then the more stamina to him! It is indeed a happy man whose first thought is the pleasure of his partner—for she will return it manifold.

With the benefit of the Danaan worldview we can expand even upon all this, to extend these insights to all male humans, of whatever gender: to elucidate that core source of meaning in the Life of each male of all species, all conditions.

The source of meaning in every male's life is his love for The Female. That love may be expressed in his ardent devotion to one Partner; or his dedication to Women, their rights and the life, health and freedom of their children; or his devotion to the One: She who is Liberty Herself.

This love for The Female, unconditional, freely given and freely received, is the source of all males' true happiness, and their eminent empowerment as a great and positive force for Life and Liberty.

ATHENADORUS

On Fatherhood:
an Honorable Estate

Men learn best by example—rôles, and their expectations and requirements, they learn from their fathers, grandfathers, siblings and friends: from role models.

This is most apparent when one observes the patterns in how fathers act with their children, towards the mother of those children and towards the other members of their families and communities, and the way those actions and attitudes mirror those of the adult men of their youths.

If I were asked to describe an exemplary figure, a father from whom others might take a positive lesson, I could do no better than to refer them to my own father.

He was not a public figure; he belonged to no large organizations; he was not wealthy in physical goods. Yet more people came to his funeral to pay their respects to him than had ever attended a remembrance service at that long-lived mortuary.

His life had not been easy. Infantile paralysis at 11 months had taken the sight from his left eye. His mother had been hooked on morphine by a quack country doctor; her addiction caused emotional and financial pain and distress within his family. That same doctor had packed the passage between his mother's mouth and her sinus that had opened when he pulled one of her cuspid ("eye") teeth, so that it healed without closing. This passage had to be cleaned and repacked every day for the final 60 or so years of her life. While my grandfather was able, he performed this unpalatable duty, but when he got older, my father took over more and more, relying as well on help from his one surviving brother.

After various jobs, he became an independent carpenter. In the South of those days no one ever considered unionization, so he was uninsured and unbuffered against adversity. When I was in the first grade a palette of sheetrock fell on his leg and broke it. Money was tight, but there was never a question of love or dedication.

Later in life, he was diagnosed with a pituitary tumor. He celebrated his 67th birthday just before the surgery, and was up, walking in the hall and chatting to people the day after the brain surgery. The tumor was benign; he was indomitable.

Because of the difficulties involved in making a living during the Depression, and in the rural South throughout his life, he held as honorable all who worked with dedication and competence, no matter how menial the task might be adjudged by others. One of his sayings was, "Always turn a good hand." He held that if you put your heart into your task, your task will grow lighter, and your heart will grow fuller.

He tried to be polite at all times; he was genuinely respectful. Because he brought his level-headed best to any circumstance, he seemed to be always at peace with himself. The first time he came to my mother's family home to court her, one evening in the middle of the week, her father got mad and ran him off, telling him that if he was an honorable man, he'd come by on Sunday so he could be seen in the light of day and let them meet him when there wasn't work to be done. My father showed up that next Sunday afternoon—and he was soon thereafter my grandfather's favorite son-in-law. His life, by example, demonstrated that there is no bad situation that cannot be conquered by a good attitude.

He was not 'perfect'; all are constrained by circumstances, and not all circumstances allow the best results. But at the end of his life he was what he had always sought to be: a good man.

I could mention other men who have demonstrated laudable determination and dedication. Brothers, brothers-in-law, nephews, cousins and friends—many are those who have exhibited praiseworthy attitudes and demeanor. Several of these were influenced by my father's example; yet each in turn has discovered the serene fulfillment of being able to 'turn a good hand'.

ATHENADORUS

APPENDIX
DANAAN CALENDAR COMPUTATIONS

The Danaan Calendar is based on the Solar Tropical Year (in which one year equals 365.24219878 days) and is easily convertible to and from the Julian Day standard, to allow conversion between it and most other calendar systems presently in use.

Although year conversions can be done for all years, Longer Danaan Year Exact conversions, *i.e.*, complete date conversions, are limited to dates beginning in EY 4.6310 [4713 BCE]; such calculations should be done on the shorter year format, without the demarcating dot '.'.

The Julian Day value used in the calculations is that of UTC 00:00:00, time of the start of the day. Also, for ease of calculation, *Yevoa* is represented as "month 14", day 1, and *Anisosa* as "month 14", day 2 in the following explanation. (Use of binary-coded decimal operations is preferred over those using floating point.)

Using these definitions:
    Danaan Calendar Base = 46310
    Danaan Epoch = 30.5

To calculate the Julian Day from a Danaan Date, follow these steps:
1. subtract the Danaan Calendar Base from the Danaan Year
2. multiply by the (high-precision) Solar Tropical Year
3. add (Danaan Month - 1) * 28
4. add the Danaan Day value
5. subtract 0.5 to adjust for the Julian Day's noon-centering
6. add the Danaan Epoch
7. get the floor of the result of Step 6 and add the 0.5 noon-centering

To calculate the Danaan Date from a Julian Day, follow these steps:
1. subtract the Danaan epoch from the Julian Day
2. divide by the (high-precision) Solar Tropical Year value
3. add the Danaan Calendar Base to the integer result of Step 2, giving the Danaan Year for "EY" notation
4. take the fractional result of Step 2's division and multiply by the Solar Tropical Year to get the number of days
5. divide by 28 to get the number of months
6. add one to the integer portion of Step 5 to get the Danaan Month
7. one plus the integer of [the fractional result of Step 5's division times 28] gives the Danaan day of the month (if the result of Step 6 is the 'non-month' 14, day 1 will be *Yevoa*; day 2 will be *Anisosa*)

Example calculations:

Using EY 5.3014.II.18 (February 7, 1992 CE), date of the signing of the Maastricht Treaty of the European Union, as the data:
(*using BCD math to avoid floating-point errors*)

Calculating the Julian Day value from Danaan Date, **EY 5.3014.II.18**:
1. subtract the Danaan Calendar Base from the Danaan Year
   `53014 - 46310 = 6704`
2. multiply by the (high-precision) Solar Tropical Year
   `6704 * 365.24219878 = 2448583.70`
3. add (Danaan Month - 1) * 28
   `2448583.70 + ((2 - 1) * 28) = 2448611.70`
4. add the Danaan Day value
   `2448611.70 + 18 = 2448629.70`
5. subtract 0.5 to adjust for the Julian Day's noon-centering
   `2448629.70 - 0.5 = 2448629.20`
6. add the Danaan Epoch
   `2448629.20 + 30.5 = 2448659.70`
7. get the floor of the result of Step 6 and add the 0.5 for noon-centering
   `floor(2448659.70) + 0.5 = JD `**`2448659.5`**

Calculating the Danaan Date from Julian Day **2448659.5**:
1. subtract the Danaan epoch from the Julian Day
   `2448659.5 - 30.5 = 2448629`
2. divide by the (high-precision) Solar Tropical Year value
   `2448629 / 365.24219878 = 6704.1240`
3. add the Danaan Calendar Base to the integer result of §2, giving the Danaan Year for "EY" notation
   `6704 + 46310 = 53014` → **EY 5.3014**
4. take the fractional result of Step 2's division and multiply by the Solar Tropical Year to get the number of days
   `0.1240 * 365.24219878 = 45.299378880`
5. divide by 28 to get the number of months
   `45.299378880 / 28 = 1.617834960`
6. add one to the integer portion of Step 5 to get the Danaan Month
   `1 + 1 = 2` → **EY 5.3014.II**
7. one plus the integer of the fractional result of Step 5's division times 28 gives the Danaan day of the month (if the result of Step 6 is the 'non-month' 14, day 1 will be *Yevoa*; day 2 will be *Anisosa*)
   `int(0.617834960 * 28) + 1 = 18` → **EY 5.3014.II.18**

www.ingramcontent.com/pod-product-compliance
Lightning Source LLC
LaVergne TN
LVHW051825080426
835512LV00018B/2729